School Psychology Ethics in the Workplace

School Psychology Ethics in the Workplace introduces a pragmatic and user-friendly model that helps readers become proficient ethical decision-makers using the 2020 National Association of School Psychologists (NASP) ethical code and to critically engage the ethical standards and work through ethical dilemmas that often occur in school and clinical settings.

This book provides an overview of NASP's latest *Principles for Professional Ethics.* It introduces readers to various ethical codes related to psychology, the importance of having ethical codes, the limitations of ethical codes, and an ethical decision-making model that accounts for multicultural and social justice issues. Over 100 ethical case studies are presented in the text that specifically relate to NASP's *Principles for Professional Ethics.* Readers are provided step-by-step directions on how to use the ethical decision-making model when problem-solving each case scenario.

School psychology graduate students and their instructors will find this guide invaluable for learning NASP's new ethical code and for being prepared for situations school psychologists are likely to experience in practice.

Dr. Daniel F. McCleary is an associate professor at Stephen F. Austin State University. He is the training director of the M.A. school psychology program within the Department of Human Services and Educational Leadership, where he has been teaching ethics since 2014. Dr. McCleary has been published in peer-reviewed international and national journals. Prior to working in academia, he served as a school psychologist in public schools and as a psychologist in private practice.

Dr. Jillian Dawes is an assistant professor at The Citadel, where she teaches students in psychology graduate and undergraduate programs. Dr. Dawes includes instruction on ethics and decision-making activities across psychology courses, notably focusing on informed consent and assent, research ethics, and direct service provision. Dr. Dawes' research, training, and practice interests focus on efficient learning and behavior change using a problem-solving model.

School Psychology Ethics in the Workplace

Daniel F. McCleary and Jillian Dawes

Routledge
Taylor & Francis Group
NEW YORK AND LONDON

Cover image: Getty Image

First published 2023
by Routledge
605 Third Avenue, New York, NY 10158

and by Routledge
4 Park Square, Milton Park, Abingdon, Oxon, OX14 4RN

Routledge is an imprint of the Taylor & Francis Group, an informa business

Library of Congress Cataloging-in-Publication Data
Names: McCleary, Daniel F., author. | Dawes, Jillian, author.
Title: School psychology ethics in the workplace / Daniel F. McCleary, Jillian Dawes.
Description: New York, NY : Routledge, 2023. | Includes bibliographical references and index.
Identifiers: LCCN 2022021323 (print) | LCCN 2022021324 (ebook) | ISBN 9781032227399 (hardback) | ISBN 9781032227382 (paperback) | ISBN 9781003273950 (ebook)
Subjects: LCSH: School psychologists—Professional ethics—United States. | School psychology—Moral and ethical aspects—United States. | National Association of School Psychologists. Principles for professional ethics.
Classification: LCC LB3013.6 .M368 2023 (print) | LCC LB3013.6 (ebook) | DDC 371.7/13—dc23/eng/20220719
LC record available at https://lccn.loc.gov/2022021323
LC ebook record available at https://lccn.loc.gov/2022021324

ISBN: 978-1-032-22739-9 (hbk)
ISBN: 978-1-032-22738-2 (pbk)
ISBN: 978-1-003-27395-0 (ebk)

DOI: 10.4324/9781003273950

Typeset in NewBaskerville
by Apex CoVantage, LLC

Access the [Support Material]: www.routledge.com/9781032227382

Contents

1 Introduction to Professional Ethics in School Psychology

A Brief History of Ethics

Definition and Origin of Ethics

The study of ethics was first proposed by ancient philosophers considering what were the "right" behaviors of people. Originally, discussion of ethics was tied up with morality and personal character, with those behaving unethically said to have a character flaw or to be immoral (Freeman, 1999). Interpretations of behaviors were "good" and "bad," and one's actions defined their morality. From this ancient discourse on ethics, we now have laws, human and animal rights, and other policies for how we are expected to behave in society, as well as professional codes of ethics. While differences in ethical behavior may be observed across various cultures, religions, and even individuals, modern ethical codes and laws are designed to apply equally to those with different beliefs and values in order to uphold the common good (Tyson, 2019).

Over time, the study of ethics has focused less on developing theories of ethics and more on developing principles, codes, and laws that can be applied to govern and guide individuals. The modern definition of ethics includes terms like "a set of moral principles," "the principles of conduct governing an individual or a group," and "a set of moral issues or aspects" (Merriam-Webster, n.d.), which define ethics as collections of principles primarily designed to govern the behavior of individuals. As can be seen in these definitions, ethics remain tightly connected to morality; although we begin to see a separation between two types of ethics: moral, or personal, ethics and professional ethics.

Moral Ethics and Professional Ethics

According to the Center for the Study of Ethics in the Professions at Illinois Institute of Technology (1994), an occupation becomes a profession when two criteria are met: members of the profession share the same occupation with a moral purpose, and members create and follow a set of standards for the work in their profession. Given these criteria, many occupations in the social services, including school psychology, may be considered professions. The standards for professional work include, but may not be limited to, codes for professional ethics. For example, the National Association of School Psychologists (NASP) has developed both standards for practice (Practice Model) and ethical standards (*Principles for Professional Ethics*; NASP, 2020).

As discussed in the previous section, the study of ethics is entwined with morality and character, and one's own moral compass can be described as personal ethics. Moral ethics apply to many areas, such as laws, religion, and individual, cultural, and societal values. Moral ethics applied across all areas of human behavior, with the expectation that

DOI: 10.4324/9781003273950-1

professionals would utilize their morals, or personal ethics, in the decisions they made in their work. Many events over time, where individuals evidenced personal ethics were not consistent with professional expectations, or not sufficient to govern professional behavior, led to the development and continued modification of codes for professional ethics (Freeman, 1999). Although professional ethics are frequently grounded in the morality of the culture and society in which they are developed, there is not always an explicit link between professional ethics and morality (Pettifor, 2004). There are times when personal ethics and professional ethics may be at odds, necessitating professionals to consider the best course of action to satisfy all requirements. Additionally, while there are similarities across professional codes of ethics, professional ethics deal with the behaviors of individuals working in specific professions, and no professional code applies to all working professionals. Rather, each profession develops and enforces its own code(s) of ethics, leading those working under multiple credentials or roles to be knowledgeable of and practice within the boundaries of more than one code of professional ethics.

Ethics in Psychology and Education

One significant similarity across codes of professional ethics, particularly those whose professions provide a social service, is the protection of human rights. This protection applies to all humans across the lifespan and other individual characteristics, including race, ethnicity, sexuality, gender, disability, and more. Within education and psychology, child rights are of particular concern, as the purpose of education and related services is to promote the welfare of children (Nastasi & Naser, 2014). Related to the rights of humans is the inclusion of protective standards for individuals receiving psychological and educational services. Nearly universally, professional codes of ethics across psychology include standards for doing good, doing no harm, respecting the autonomy of individuals served, and promoting justice and equity, as a result of the 1948 *Universal Declaration of Human Rights* (Pettifor, 2004; United Nations, 1948). Given the similarities across the standards in many of the psychological sciences, some, including the European Federation of Psychologists Association and the Canadian Psychological Association, have proposed a universal code of ethics in the practice of psychology, which individual nations or organizations could adopt and modify to fit within the societal expectations of their regions. Criticisms of this attempt include that the foundations of many existing ethical codes in psychology are rooted in Western culture and may not apply universally (Pettifor, 2004).

We begin to see contrasts across codes for professional psychology ethics in the specific ethical concerns within areas of practice. Although many activities are similar across psychology training and practice, there are some differences. For example, school psychologists may be more likely to engage in interprofessional collaboration, often working in teams of other educational professionals to provide services to children and their families. Therefore, specific ethical standards related to the collaboration and consultation with other professionals are more detailed in school psychology ethical codes than in other areas of psychology. Additionally, school psychologists primarily work in public school settings (85%; NASP, 2021b). Education professionals have additional professional ethics for school psychologists to consider, often being provided by each state's department of education.

Advantages and Disadvantages of Professional Codes of Ethics

The existence of a professional code of ethics is advantageous for the field in that it protects the public, upholds the public's trust in the profession by providing a mechanism to understand what one can expect from the profession and by providing an avenue to hold a provider accountable, demonstrates the field is interested in the health of the public by holding its members accountable, and signifies the maturity of the field (Behnke & Jones, 2012; Bersoff & Koeppl, 1993; Williams et al., 2008). Ethical codes also possess several inherent disadvantages. First, they are limited in that they must be sufficiently broad (a.k.a. vague) to address a variety of situations without being overly restrictive, thus preventing advancements within the field (Bersoff, 1994). Second, codes must be specific enough to provide guidance to individual situations. This can result in several standards applying to the same ethical dilemma and standards that appear to conflict with each other and with the law (Bersoff & Koeppl, 1993; Haas & Malouf, 2005; Jacob et al., 2022; Koocher & Keith-Spiegel, 2016). Third, ethical codes are reactive in nature. Ethical codes are routinely revised, and the wording of each standard is carefully considered to address advances in the field without being overly prohibitive. However, this reactive stance, responding to issues that have arisen in practice and in the courts that go beyond the specificity of the current ethical code, means that the code is likely outdated by the time it is published (Bersoff & Koeppl, 1993; Jacob et al., 2022; Welfel, 2012). Fifth, given the aforementioned limitations of ethical codes, the school psychologist is responsible for being well versed in the meaning and interpretation of the ethical codes that apply to the profession and making the determination of how the various standards direct the practitioner's response to their specific dilemma (NASP, 2020). Ethical dilemmas are considered dilemmas because there are often multiple ways to ethically respond to the situation and multiple unethical ways of addressing the dilemma (Williams & Monahon, 2018). When confronted with several choices for resolving an ethical dilemma, the school psychologist should employ an ethical decision-making model, consult with other professionals, and/or seek supervision (NASP, 2020).

NASP *Principles for Professional Ethics*

In 1974, NASP adopted its first ethical code, *Principles for Professional Ethics.* The code was revised and adopted again in 1984, 1992, 1997, 2000, 2010, and most recently in 2020 (NASP, 2020). The creation of a professional ethical code is a significant milestone for a profession, indicating the maturation of the field (Chalk et al., 1980; Jacob et al., 2022). It is advantageous for a field to create enforceable standards so the field can police itself rather than rely on people outside the profession, such as lawyers and judges, who are not familiar enough with the intricacies and nuances of a field, particularly one as complex as school psychology, to identify potential unintended consequences a regulation may have on other aspects of professional functioning (Jacob et al., 2022).

The NASP *Principles for Professional Ethics* includes a description of its purpose, information on how to use the ethical principles, and a list of definitions used in the code. The code itself is categorized by four broad themes that are aspirational: Respecting the Dignity and Rights of All Persons; Professional Competence and Responsibility; Honesty and Integrity in Professional Relationships; and Responsibility to Schools, Families, Communities, The Profession, and Society. Each theme is then organized by Guiding Principles and their enforceable standards. The Code concludes with a topic index for the ethical principles.

Key Changes to the 2020 Principles for Professional Ethics

The 2020 *Principles for Professional Ethics* was revised in a multitude of ways. Our purpose here is merely to highlight some of those changes, not to provide an exhaustive list of the changes. The most visually recognizable change pertains to the addition of a topic index for the ethical principles. This section, located at the end of the code, lists all standards related to a specific concept (e.g., confidentiality, supervision, social justice) and provides a hyperlink for each standard listed that will automatically redirect the reader to that specific standard, making it much easier for the user to search and find relevant standards. This topical guide also makes more explicit how seemingly general statements can apply to specific circumstances. For example, Standard III.5.I Private Versus Professional Conduct contains no mention of social media posts but is listed under the topical heading of Social Media, suggesting that the content of one's social media posts on their personal account may cross into the realm of their professional life. An example would be if a practitioner were to post about events that happened at the workplace with clients or students and the person included identifying information, even if names were not used. Another visually recognizable change was the inclusion of narrative titles that accompany each standard. Previously standards were recognized simply by their standard number (e.g., Standard I.1.3); whereas they are now accompanied by a title for ease of reference (e.g., Standard I.1.3 Seeking Informed Consent). Much like the topical index, the inclusion of standard titles makes it easier for practitioners to skim through the code to find the information they are looking for. However, we caution graduate students and practitioners to not solely rely on this method for identifying relevant standards. The code should be read in its entirety each year to know what titles to look for when skimming through in the middle of a potentially ethically compromised situation.

Standard II.2.2. Progress Monitoring was revised to clarify that school psychologists are responsible for ensuring the effectiveness of interventions, whether they are the ones implementing the intervention or not. Related to providing reactive guidance but with anticipation for future advancements, NASP revised Guiding Principle II.3 Responsible Assessment and Intervention Practices to broaden its scope to encompass a variety of technological advancements related to assessment and intervention. For example, the guiding principle is now written to include computer-assisted digital formats, virtual reality, distance assessment and telehealth intervention, and "any other assessment or intervention modality" (NASP, 2020, p. 46). Standard II.4.5 Test Protocols was also substantially changed to provide more explicit guidance on the rights of parents to view their child's responses on protocols and other assessments regardless of the test publisher's interests. Standard III.1.4 Graduate Programs was added to regulate descriptions graduate programs provide to the public that are factual and not misleading. For example, graduate programs that are not NASP approved should not advertise that the program is aligned with NASP standards. Standard III.5.2 Separation of Personal Beliefs was also added to clarify that all "decisions, recommendations, and activities are guided by the evidence base and by best practices" (NASP, 2020, p. 52). This revision highlights the need for the provision of services founded on evidence-based practices and not religious, spiritual, or personal belief systems (i.e., professional ethics v. moral ethics).

Related Codes of Professional Ethics

As previously discussed, school psychologists may work in various settings and under more than one credential. For this reason, it is necessary for school psychologists to have a strong working knowledge of each of these codes for professional ethics, so that they can synthesize and address each in their professional practice. There are standards where each code overlaps and no modifications are needed; however, there are also discrepancies between some of the codes, which school psychologists will need to consider when making decisions. The following sections, although not an exhaustive list, summarize a few of the relevant codes for professional ethics in psychology.

American Psychological Association

The American Psychological Association (APA) has provided the *Ethical Principles of Psychologists and Code of Conduct* (the Ethics Code) to guide psychologists in their practice. The Ethics Code includes an Introduction, Preamble, and five General Principles. Additionally, specific Ethical Standards are included, with the intent to address specific issues that may arise in the practice of psychology (APA, 2017). Like many codes of ethics, APA's Ethics Code is not exhaustive and allows room for interpretation and professional judgment. The Ethics Code applies to all members of the APA in their professional practice of psychology, regardless of credentialing, specialty area, or practice setting.

The five General Principles of the Ethics Code have been adopted by other professional organizations' codes of ethics, and include Beneficence and Nonmaleficence, Fidelity and Responsibility, Integrity, Justice, and Respect for People's Rights and Dignity (APA, 2017). Specific Ethical Standards address issues that arise in resolving ethical issues, competence, human relations, privacy and confidentiality, advertising and public statements, record keeping and fees, education and training, research and publication, assessment, and therapy. Within each of these areas are specific guidelines for behaving ethically in the professional practice of psychology.

Canadian Psychological Association

The Canadian Psychological Association (CPA) has published the *Canadian Code of Ethics for Psychologists*, which is currently in its fourth edition (CPA, 2017). This code includes a preamble that includes guidance for using the code in ethical decision-making. In contrast to the APA Ethics Code discussed before, the CPA code has incorporated all ethical standards under four primary standards. These standards include Respect for the Dignity of Persons and Peoples, Responsible Caring, Integrity in Relationships, and Responsibility to Society. Under each standard are a values statement and the specific ethical standards related to the overarching principle. The values statement is a narrative of the values and morals that contribute to the specific standards that follow, whereas the specific standards are action-oriented descriptions of ethical behavior in the practice of psychology.

International School Psychology Association

The International School Psychology Association's (ISPA) *Code of Ethics* provides an introduction to the general purpose of the *Code of Ethics*, particularly noting that it does not replace the national codes that have been adopted in the locations of psychologists' practice (International School Psychology Association, 2021). There is additional overlap between APA and ISPA in the general principles, named Prevailing Ethical Principles in the ISPA *Code of Ethics*, with principles in the following areas being adopted: Beneficence and Nonmaleficence, Competence, Fidelity and Responsibility, Integrity, Respect for People's Rights and Dignity, and Social Justice.

Following the introduction and general principles, ISPA's *Code of Ethics* introduces professional standards in the following areas: professional responsibilities, confidentiality, professional growth, and professional limitations. Each of these areas addresses potential issues in the practice of school psychology. The following section, Professional Practices, covers specific standards in the practice of school psychology, including professional relationships with children, colleagues and other professionals, assessment, and research.

Universal Declaration of Ethical Principles for Psychologists

As noted previously, there is significant overlap between ethical codes within the field of psychology and the *Universal Declaration of Ethical Principles for Psychologists* (UDEPP; International Union of Psychological Science, 2008) is no exception. The UDEPP was adopted by the Assembly of the International Union of Psychological Science and the Board of Directors of the International Association of Applied Psychology in July 2008. The UDEPP includes a preamble describing the moral framework and purpose of the code, followed by four principles. These principles, again, will be familiar to readers.

The first Principle is Respect for the Dignity of Persons and Peoples, which addresses the rights of individuals served, including dignity, respect for diversity, informed consent, privacy, fairness and justice, and others. The second Principle is Competent Caring for the Well-Being of Persons and Peoples, which includes maximizing benefits, minimizing harm, developing and maintaining competence, and self-awareness. Principle III is Integrity, and refers to honest, truthful, open, and accurate communication about psychological practices, as well as avoiding exploitation and conflicts of interest. The final Principle, Professional and Scientific Responsibilities to Society, includes psychology's responsibility to increase scientific knowledge through research, training, and commentary, as well as the responsibility to uphold ethical standards.

Behavior Analysis Certification Board

The Behavior Analyst Certification Board (BACB®) has provided the *Professional and Ethical Compliance Code for Behavior Analysts* (the Code; BACB, 2020). This set of standards has recently been updated, and the *Ethics Code for Behavior Analysts* went into effect in January 2022 (BACB, 2020). Like the previously discussed codes of ethics, the BACB code includes an introduction, which discusses the scope, application, and enforcement of the code, as well as core principles. The core principles should sound familiar, as they are similar to those discussed in previous codes, stating that behavior analysts should: Benefit Others; Treat Others with Compassion, Dignity, and Respect; Behave with Integrity; and Ensure their Competence.

Following these sections, the Code provides Ethics Standards in sections, which are specific to issues that may arise in practice. The sections of the Ethics Standards include guidance for behavior analysts' responsibilities as a professional, in practice, to clients and stakeholders, to supervisees and trainees, in public statements, and in research, with specific standards addressed under each section. Of note, the BACB Code is written in a way that is prescriptive, clear, and leaves little up to professional judgment. Much of the code is written in behavioral terms, with expectations clearly defined and ethical actions listed in each section.

School Psychologists and Multiple Responsibilities

Over time, school psychologists' roles have expanded to include more than the original "evaluator" role in schools. School psychologists are now trained to provide assessment, prevention, intervention, consultation, and other mental health supports and services to individuals and systems in public schools and other settings (NASP, 2021a). Due to this expanded training and service provision, school psychologists may, at times, operate under multiple roles and credentials. For example, a doctoral-level school psychologist may be a certified or licensed school psychologist in public schools while also maintaining a private practice under a psychology license. As another example, a school psychologist may also have completed behavior-analytic coursework and supervised experiences during their school psychology training, resulting in dual certification as a school psychologist and behavior analyst. In each of these examples, the school psychologist would be operating under multiple credentials and codes of ethics. For this reason, school psychologists need to understand the overlap, as well as the dissimilarities between all ethical codes under which they are bound. While similarities between the codes of ethics have been noted multiple times in this chapter, there may be times when codes you must follow differ from each other. There may also be times when you are not sure which ethical code applies to your practice.

In general, the NASP Standards apply to members of NASP and those working as credentialed school psychologists in school settings. The APA Ethics Code applies to all members of the APA. Additionally, many states' psychology licensure boards have adopted this code, so that all psychologists with a state license are bound by APA's Ethics Code. Furthermore, many school psychology state organizations require their members to adhere to their respective national organization's ethical code. School districts, as per terms of employment may also require school psychologists to adhere to the NASP *Principles for Professional Ethics.* The BACB Code applies to those who are credentialed as a Board Certified Behavior Analyst (BCBA®) or a Board Certified Assistant Behavior Analyst (BCaBA®). A separate code applies to behavioral service providers who operate under consistent supervision, Registered Behavior Technicians (RBT®). However, the UDEPP and ISPA *Code of Ethics* are aspirational. Nonetheless, a practitioner choosing to forego paying dues to be a member of professional organizations and carefully selecting both a state and an employer that does not require adherence to an ethical code will likely still be held accountable in a court of law when their actions are weighed against the standard of care set forth by the field of school psychology as evidenced by expert testimony from those within the field and by the relevant professional ethical codes (Jacobs et al., 2022).

When compared to the NASP *Principles for Professional Ethics* (NASP, 2020), there can be seen significant overlap in general standards and areas covered across each of the discussed ethical codes; however, there are times when the codes will differ and may be in direct opposition to each other or legal statutes. In these events, school psychologists must be familiar with each of the codes that apply to the current issue. General guidance is to follow the code that is the most stringent. For example, if one code says records should be maintained for five years and another says seven years, the best decision would be to maintain records for seven years, as this meets the requirements for both codes. When an ethical code is at odds with a law, school psychologists should follow the law if it does not violate basic human rights but should document and report how this decision is at odds with the code of ethics under which the school psychologists' practice is covered (APA, 2017; NASP, 2020). These instances may present opportunities to advocate for changes in either the law or the ethical code.

An additional consideration: school psychologists often work with individuals who are not governed by the same ethical codes as they are. These individuals may have a different, or even no, ethical code under which they must operate and may have little-to-no knowledge of or experience with ethical codes related to the practice of school psychology. To this end, it is possible, and research shows, school psychologists may be advised or encouraged to act outside of their ethical code (Helton & Ray, 2009). School psychologists ultimately serve in the difficult multiple positions of advocate, service provider, and school employee, while needing to navigate their ethical responsibilities in each role and educating others about their ethical responsibilities.

Summary

Of the ethical codes covered in this chapter, some are specific to role and setting, while others are more general. Each ethical code directly applies to those who are either members of the organization or are credentialed by an organization that has adopted the code of that organization. Sometimes, part of your practice may be covered only by one ethical code, and sometimes it will be covered by multiple codes, which may not always overlap perfectly. School psychologists must know the ethical code(s) under which their practice is covered, follow the code(s), and help others to follow the code(s). School psychologists must also consider their personal ethics and how these might affect their ability to hold themselves and others to codes for professional ethics, while not applying their personal ethics to those who have not adopted those same values.

As described in this chapter, many ethical codes include vague language and guidance to address multiple aspects of practice in general themes. Given the scope of the practice of psychology, a specific list of standards for all aspects of practice and potential ethical issues would require a lengthy document that would need to be updated constantly to keep up with new areas of practice. This is an unlikely undertaking, which means school psychologists will need to be able to read, interpret, and apply the code(s) to their specific areas of practice. The purpose of this book is to provide school psychologists practicing in a variety of settings with a guide for, and practice with, making ethical decisions using the NASP *Principles for Professional Ethics* and any overlapping ethical codes. In the next chapter, we will discuss the use of consultation and collaboration within an ethical problem-solving model to improve ethical decision-making.

Reference List

American Psychological Association. (2017, January 1). *Ethical principles of psychologists and code of conduct.* www.apa.org/ethics/code/ethics-code-2017.pdf

Behavior Analyst Certification Board. (2020). *Ethics code for behavior analysts.* www.bacb.com/ethics-information/ethics-codes/

Behnke, S. H., & Jones, S. E. (2012). Ethics and ethics codes for psychologists. In S. J. Knapp, M. C. Gottlieb, M. M. Handelsman, & L. D. VandeCreek (Eds.), *APA handbook of ethics in psychology* (Vol. 1, pp. 43–74). American Psychological Association. https://doi.org/10.1037/13271-002

Bersoff, D. N. (1994). Explicit ambiguity: The 1992 ethics code as an oxymoron. *Professional Psychology: Research and Practice, 25*(4), 382–387. https://doi.org/10.1037/0735-7028.25.4.382

Bersoff, D. N., & Koeppl, P. M. (1993). The relation between ethical codes and moral principles. *Ethics and Behavior, 3*(3–4), 345–357. https://doi.org/10.1080/10508422.1993.9652112

Canadian Psychological Association. (2017, January 1). *Canadian code of ethics for psychologists* (4th ed.). https://cpa.ca/docs/File/Ethics/CPA_Code_2017_4thEd.pdf

Chalk, R., Frankel, M. S., & Chafer, S. B. (1980). *AAAS professional ethics project.* American Association for the Advancement of Science.

Freeman, N. K. (1999). Morals and character: The foundations of ethics and professionalism. *The Educational Forum, 63*(1), 30–36. https://doi.org/10.1080/00131729808984384

Haas, L., & Malouf, J. L. (2005). *Keeping up the good work: A practitioner's guide to mental health ethics* (4th ed.). Professional Resources Press.

Helton, G. B., & Ray, B. A. (2009). Administrative pressures to practice unethically: Research and suggested strategies. *Ethical Human Psychology and Psychiatry, 11*(2), 112–119. https://doi.org/10.1891/1559-4343.11.2.112

Illinois Institute of Technology Center for the Study of Ethics in the Professions. (1994). *Professional ethics.* https://ethics.iit.edu/teaching/professional-ethics

International School Psychology Association. (2021). *Code of ethics.* https://www.ispaweb.org/wp-content/uploads/2021/07/ISPA-Code-of-Ethics-2021.pdf

International Union of Psychological Science. (2008, July). *Universal declaration of ethical principles for psychologists.* www.iupsys.net/about/governance/universal-declaration-of-ethical-principles-for-psychologists.html

Jacob, S. (2014). Best practices in ethical school psychological practice. In P. L. Harrison & A. Thomas (Eds.), *Best practices in school psychology: Foundations* (pp. 437–448). NASP.

Jacob, S., Decker, D. M., Lugg, E. T., & Diamond, E. (2022). *Ethics and law for school psychologists* (8th ed.). John Wiley & Sons, Inc.

Koocher, G. P., & Keith-Spiegel, P. (2016). *Ethics in psychology and the mental health professions Standards and cases* (4th ed.). Oxford University Press.

Merriam-Webster. (n.d.). *Ethic.* www.merriam-webster.com/dictionary/ethics

Nastasi, B. K., & Naser, S. (2014). Child rights as a framework for advancing professional standards for practice, ethics, and professional development in school psychology. *School Psychology International, 35*(1), 36–49. https://doi.org/10.1177/0143034313512409

National Association of School Psychologists. (2020). *The professional standards of the National Association of School Psychologists.* Retrieved May 1, 2021, from www.nasponline.org/x55315.xml

National Association of School Psychologists. (2021a). *Who are school psychologists.* www.nasponline.org/about-school-psychology/who-are-school-psychologists

National Association of School Psychologists. (2021b). *Workforce & salary information.* www.nasponline.org/about-school-psychology/workforce-and-salary-information

Pettifor, J. L. (2004). Professional ethics across national boundaries. *European Psychologist, 9*(4), 264–272. https:doi.org/10.1027/1016-9040.9.4.264

Tyson, J. M. (2019). Morals, ethics, and laws: What commonalities remain? *Liberty University Law Review, 14*(1).

United Nations. (1948). *Universal declaration of human rights.* Retrieved February 10, 2022, from www.un.org/en/about-us/universal-declaration-of-human-rights

Welfel, W. R. (2012). Teaching ethics: Models, methods, and challenges. In S. J. Knapp, M. C. Gottlieb, M. M. Handelsman, & L. D. VandeCreek (Eds.), *APA handbook of ethics in psychology* (Vol. 2, pp. 277–305). American Psychological Association. https://doi.org/10.1037/13272-014

Williams, B. B., Armistead, L., & Jacob, S. (2008). *Professional ethics for school psychologists: A problem-solving model casebook.* National Association of School Psychologists.

Williams, B. B., & Monahon, L. W. (2018). Ethical and legal foundations. In S. L. Grapin & J. H. Kranzler (Eds.), *School psychology: Professional issues and practices* (pp. 77–93). Springer.

2 Consultation and Collaboration in Ethical Problem-Solving

Introduction

We have previously discussed the sometimes-ambiguous nature of ethical dilemmas. While professional organizations are continually revising their ethical codes to address changes in expectations over time and to address any shortcomings, it would be unbelievably difficult to capture all possible ethical dilemmas in black-and-white in an ethical code. To help with generalizability, the codes tend to use loose language that applies to a variety of situations. However, with this lack of explicit guidance, school psychologists may find themselves questioning whether an ethical dilemma has occurred and how best to respond to the situation, particularly in those situations where there is more room for interpretation. This may be especially true for early career school psychologists and those who have not engaged in ethical problem-solving before.

The authors of this book recommend collaborative ethical problem-solving for all dilemmas, but especially in those situations where you might question the most appropriate response. In this chapter, we will discuss the use of and evidence for collaborative ethical problem-solving in school psychology and other fields. As you will see next, there is little research literature examining the role of consultation and collaboration in ethical problem-solving, especially in school psychology. Despite this lack of evidence, the authors believe other areas of research supporting collaborative efforts in problem-solving (such as with school-based data review teams and peer mentorship during graduate training) can be generalized to improve interpretation of ethical codes, consideration of ethical dilemmas and potentially-contributing factors, and the creation of a response to the dilemma. For example, the authors have experienced first-hand, while creating the very scenarios available to you in this book, the utility of having another person's perspective in interpreting ethical codes and considering the best responses for problem-solving. Consultation can also be a way to engage in ethical problem-solving with someone with more, or less, experience than you to build competence and provide/receive supervision. We will also include a description of peer and collegial support used across graduate training and how you might engage in continued use of peer support across your career as a school psychologist.

Collaborative Ethical Problem-Solving

Collaborative ethical problem-solving is part of the standard of care in many helping professions. For example, medical professionals often engage in rounds, where multiple professionals contribute to problem-solving difficult cases, including ethical dilemmas. Despite school psychology's common use of cohort models and peer mentors in graduate training and encouragement of participation in school-based problem-solving teams with other professionals, we were able to find very little (i.e., no) research on the use of consultation and

DOI: 10.4324/9781003273950-2

collaboration in ethical problem-solving by school psychologists. That being said, many of the current ethical decision-making models advocated in school psychology do recommend, at some level, consultation with peers and colleagues (Lasser & Klose, 2007). We will first discuss how collaborative ethical problem-solving looks in other fields, followed by what we know and next directions for ethical problem-solving in school psychology.

Other Fields

Medical Care

There are several examples of ethical problem-solving collaboration in medical and healthcare settings. For example, Norway has implemented a country-wide model for systematic consultation and supports in both medical and residential nursing home settings. A fairly recent survey of nursing home staff, including both nursing staff and support employees, indicated there is both a need and desire for systematic processes for ethical problem-solving, particularly for common and frequent ethical challenges (Bollig et al., 2015). Survey respondents reported some resources that would support their ethical decision-making, including scheduled time for discussion of ethical challenges and dilemmas, meeting spaces for these discussions, as well as consultation with others—other employees, others more knowledgeable than they are, and those with professional knowledge (e.g., ethicist, lawyer). Further, survey respondents reported several areas that frequently come up as ethical challenges and dilemmas, which carry substantial overlap with the challenges faced by school psychologists, including patient autonomy and capacity for decision-making, availability of resources needed to provide adequate care, collaboration with patients and patients' families, and privacy of patients (Bollig et al., 2015).

Hospitals and other healthcare settings also typically have set meetings where ethical challenges and dilemmas may be discussed. One unique example of this is ethical rounds. Svantesson and colleagues (2008) examined a model for ethical rounds in a medical setting. In this study, a philosopher-ethicist guided doctors and nurses through ethical challenges by first ensuring understanding of the challenge, then by facilitating problem-solving discussions without providing recommendations. Doctors and nurses reported both positive and negative outcomes of the guided ethical rounds. Doctors and nurses reported that they thought deeper about the challenge and solutions because of the ethical rounds, that they liked the connection with other colleagues that derived from the group discussion process, that they were more confident in the resulting action, that they had a better understanding of their ethical and moral responsibilities, and that they felt relief after the problem-solving discussion. Doctors and nurses in this study also reported feeling alienated, being frustrated when a lack of solutions was available, and feeling resigned when it seemed as if change was not possible. Based on these findings, Svantesson and colleagues (2008) recommended that ethical rounds include a balance between three components when engaging in interdisciplinary ethical discussions: analysis of the ethical challenge or dilemma, problem-solving, and conflict resolution.

Colvin and colleagues (2012) also discussed the utility of multidisciplinary ethical problem-solving. Specifically, they discussed the contributions of social workers to medical-legal partnerships (MLPs). MLPs are a resource available to patients to intercept and prevent potential medical and legal issues in patient care. While ethical rounds focus on specific medical care issues, MLPs typically address whole-client care. For this reason, Colvin and colleagues (2012) recommend the inclusion of social workers to these teams to support the systems approach to problem-solving and service provision. One relevant recommendation they make, when considering generalizing this work to school psychology, is to consider the ethical and legal obligations of all the professionals involved. For example, if a school psychologist were to collaborate with other education professionals on an ethical dilemma, it must be noted and considered that each professional has their own ethical code and guidelines to uphold.

Further research has examined ethics consultation in psychiatric care (Haltaufderheide et al., 2021). Specifically, this work examines the experiences of clinical ethics support services (CESS). CESS are systems of support for ethical practice and decision-making, including ethics consultation services, and are used in many medical care settings. Ethics consultation within CESS may be pictured similarly to the previously discussed ethical rounds, where a philosopher-ethicist guides discussions to support understanding and problem analyses; however, within CESS, the ethicist provides more direct and consultative supports, rather than only facilitation. Interviews by Haltaufderheide and colleagues (2021) supported that CESS may be particularly helpful in acknowledging the subjectivity of ethical challenges and dilemmas and aiding in determining when ethical dilemmas have occurred. Further, CESS interviewees reported both feeling competent in ethical matters, based on their own training and experiences, and also wanting to consult with others for ethical guidance, indicating even those with ethical expertise may desire consultative problem-solving.

Supervisory Relationships

As a school psychology trainee or practitioner, you have almost certainly been part of a supervisory relationship. If you have not at this point in your studies, you will shortly. Löfström and Pyhältö (2012) discuss several ethical considerations within supervisory relationships. First, supervisory relationships are meant to provide supervisees with additional experiences to build knowledge and skills, where the supervisory relationship itself is foundational but is also embedded within the larger community (e.g., university, school, clinic). In this regard, supervisory relationships may be ideal for the process of collaborative or consultative ethical problem-solving. However, one must be aware of the power imbalance between supervisor and supervisee, particularly as it may relate to the social psychological phenomena discussed next. Relatedly, while supervisors are expected to have expert knowledge and skills and to avoid many ethical dilemmas, some data indicate identifying ethical challenges and dilemmas may be difficult for the actors/offenders in a supervisory ethical dilemma, such as that seen in the exploitation of supervisee work or providing inadequate supervision (Löfström & Pyhältö, 2012).

General Ethical Problem-Solving

In addition to setting-specific considerations in consultative and collaborative ethical problem-solving, some recommendations can be made about the process in terms of predictors of adequate ethical problem-solving and decision-making. Stenmark and colleagues (2010) studied factors predicting undergraduate students' ethical decision-making. Notably, a significant predictor of high-quality decisions was whether or not students identified the cause of the ethical problem. These findings align with the findings and recommendations of the previously discussed research in this chapter. While a single person may successfully identify the cause of an ethical problem, related fields have found that when that person is involved in the ethical problem, they may not recognize an ethical problem (Löfström & Pyhältö, 2012). Additionally, medical professionals reported better understanding of ethical challenges and dilemmas and an appreciation for the sense of connection found in collaborative ethical problem-solving discussions (Svantesson et al., 2008). Further, this finding aligns with this book's use of the selected ethical decision-making model (discussed in Chapter 3), which requires readers to first identify the ethical problem, followed by identifying contributing variables (e.g., the cause(s) of the problem).

School Psychology

While we were unable to find specific research in the school psychology literature on the use of consultation and collaboration in ethical problem-solving, many of the proposed ethical decision-making models encourage consultation with peers (Lasser & Klose, 2007). Lasser and Klose (2007) also discuss several social psychological phenomena that may contribute to interactions, events, or behaviors that ultimately result in ethical dilemmas. Many of these phenomena, such as risky shift and conformity, may also be useful for school psychologists to consider when engaging in collaborative problem-solving. Risky shift occurs when a group selects a riskier option in decision-making. For example, if a multidisciplinary team is presented with data that may not quite meet eligibility criteria, they can either opt to qualify or not qualify the student for services. Risky shift would be a tendency for the group to qualify the student for services, as this is the less conservative option. Risky shift could also occur in the ethical problem-solving process if collaborators lean away from a cautious, or conservative, approach to ethical decision-making. Conformity occurs when one or more group members pressure other group members to conform to their idea or decision. In the previous risky shift example, imagine if one or two of the team members held seniority over the other members and pressured them to agree with their eligibility decision. If the others did side with the senior team members, conformity would have occurred. When engaging in ethical problem-solving with collaborators, it may be important to consider any social power, real or perceived, that a collaborator holds and put measures in place to prevent pressure to conform.

Based on the practices and research from other fields, in combination with resources and standards in school psychology, we recommend that when engaging in consultation and collaboration, you a) maintain privacy and confidentiality according to all ethical codes you must follow, b) engage in problem-solving rather than focusing on things that cannot be changed (e.g., "admiring the problem"), c) use the collaborative relationship to consider multiple perspectives and outcomes, and d) use the process as a learning experience to improve your skills and your collaborators' skills in ethical problem-solving. Throughout this process, it is important to recognize the group or pair dynamic in order to identify and prevent any instances of risky shift, conformity, or other relevant social psychological phenomena.

Peer Support in School Psychology Training

The development of a professional network is embedded in many school psychology training programs and can be seen through the career-span. For example, the development of social media groups for professionals within a given field is a means of developing a professional network, as is the holding of conferences or conventions. In this section, we discuss ways to build professional networks, and how these networks might contribute to our competence, and use of consultation and collaboration, in ethical problem-solving.

Cohort Model

Many school psychology training programs utilize a cohort model. These models are intended to provide several benefits to students to support their success while completing their training. In a cohort model, students entering the program at the same time will take all their coursework together across their training, including completion of any field experiences. While some programs may have developed guidance for cohorts in order to maximize the benefits, each cohort will have its own strengths and areas for growth, resulting in a slightly different community across cohorts. In general, a cohort model provides social supports and opportunities for identity development to students. Within a cohort model, students will spend significant amounts of time together in classrooms, which often translates to studying, shared course resources, and collaborative problem-solving when issues arise, whether between cohort members or in other areas.

Because of these opportunities, there are several specific benefits a cohort model is thought to provide to trainees (Jackson, 2021). While spending time together in both professional training activities, cohort peers are able to observe each other engaging with course content. This can provide a model for expectations, which may lead to improved engagement across the cohort. Observing others develop professionally may also inspire cohort members to develop professional identity. Collaboration within cohorts can also lead to innovation inside and outside the classroom as a result of the different perspectives and experiences each member brings to the cohort. Finally, the benefit of a peer support system cannot be discounted. If you are reading this book, you likely are either a school psychology student or have gone through school psychology training. As a result, you are aware that school psychology is a little-known field, and you may experience close friends and family not understanding what you are learning or what you do professionally. Having a training cohort provides the opportunity to have a social support group who knows exactly what your chosen career is, experiences the demands and milestones of training with you, and understands the struggles and joys of selecting to become, training for, and ultimately working as a school psychologist.

This kind of social support is incredibly beneficial during training but can also result in an ongoing community of colleagues long after you complete your training. In fact, we encourage our graduate students to begin forming these exact types of relationships in graduate school, so they have an immediate social support system and consultation network upon graduation. One of the added benefits of annually attending school psychology conventions is meeting up with these friends within the profession and establishing new relationships with others. State association conventions are particularly helpful in this regard, given that most attendees are operating under the same state laws and, thus, can better understand the circumstances of a given situation.

Peer Mentorship

Peer mentorship is used both formally and informally in school psychology training programs. While a cohort model provides trainees with peer support from those going through the program at the same time as they are, peer mentorship typically involves a person in a more senior cohort mentoring a person in a junior cohort, often beginning during the first year of study. The mentor is able to experience a pseudo-supervisory role, where they can informally provide information, resources, and other supports to newer students, and the mentee gets the benefit of a go-to person who has already been in their shoes. Mentorship in school psychology has also extended to post-graduate practices, with organizations and workplaces offering mentorship opportunities to new hires and early career professionals.

The research literature notes several advantages of mentorship, including improved self-efficacy, productivity, and belongingness (Grapin et al., 2021). Further, mentorship has also shown a relationship between recruitment and retention of school psychology trainees, which has significant implications for the ongoing national workforce shortages of school psychologists (Grapin et al., 2021). Peer mentorship has also been established as a protective factor for recruiting and retaining diverse student populations. Peer mentorship, when provided effectively, may grant a more supportive means for diverse students to ask questions, learn hidden expectations in colleges and school psychology programs, access networking opportunities, and more (Rasheem et al., 2018).

A review by Grapin and colleagues (2021) examined the current state of the literature on mentorship in school psychology. In addition to the information presented earlier, their review indicated that many participants who had experienced mentoring continued the mentoring relationship past graduate training. This is the experience of the authors of this text, as well, who regularly speak with graduate school peers in both professional and personal contexts. As a "former" mentor, one author still receives requests for advice, feedback, and consultation from "former" mentees frequently, even after official mentoring relationships ended many years ago. Further, that author continues to reach out to those who mentored them during graduate training. Particularly in a field where many do not understand your training, competencies, and roles, having a network of peer support may have several additional benefits. For example, in addition to helping prevent isolation and burnout, the authors have also benefited from a robust peer support network fostered during graduate school by being able to call a knowledgeable colleague to discuss an important matter when time was of the essence, collaborate on a professional development presentation to enhance the scope and quality of the presentation, and collaborate on research projects, co-author publications, and even as co-workers (knowing who you will be working with can be great for recruiting).

Continued Use of Colleague Support

We previously mentioned the expansion of mentorship practices in school psychology to include early career professionals and new hires, with many workplaces and organizations providing structured mentorship opportunities. These opportunities are fantastic and can provide many benefits. However, sometimes colleague support may be as beneficial as mentorship. While mentorship provides opportunities to build on skills and learn new things, colleague support may provide more opportunities for consultation and social support. While there is limited-to-no research in this area in school psychology, anecdotal observations indicate school psychology teams and networks can provide a friendly group of people who have similar training and experiences. As this chapter is being written, the authors of this book are preparing to attend the NASP annual convention, and both are looking forward to meeting up with long-distance colleagues after a few years of only online communication. In addition to school psychology colleagues, you might also find support from those in related fields, such as special educators, school counselors, speech-language pathologists, and clinical psychologists. These individuals, while having different roles than school psychologists, work within many of the same systems and may be able to provide social support and advice just as well as a fellow school psychologist.

Summary

There are many opportunities for both formal and informal consultation and collaboration across school psychology training and careers. School psychology trainees may benefit from a cohort model, where they move through the plan of study and field experiences with the same peers, and peer mentorship, received by those in more senior cohorts. Early career school psychologists may take advantage of mentorship opportunities within the workplace or in professional organizations. Finally, ongoing mentor relationships and colleague support may provide additional benefits, particularly as related to consultation and social supports.

Throughout this book, you will be asked to work through ethical case scenarios, using the problem-solving model presented in the next chapter. Given the often-subjective nature of ethical dilemmas and concerns, and the observed benefits of consultation and collaboration in other areas, we recommend the use of collaborative ethical problem-solving. When completing the case scenarios, we suggest you work out a case scenario on your own, then collaborate with others and observe how the process, and outcome, changes. Additionally, completing the case scenarios in this manner requires you to recall the information and provides you with more opportunities to respond, which increases the likelihood you will retain the information from the ethical code (Peverly et al., 2014; Skinner et al., 2005).

Reference List

Bollig, G., Schmidt, G., Rosland, J. H., & Heller, A. (2015). Ethical challenges in nursing homes—staff's opinions and experiences with systematic ethics meetings with participation of residents' relatives. *Scandinavian Journal of Caring Sciences, 29*(4), 810–823. https://doi.org/10.1111/scs.12213

Colvin, J. D., Nelson, B., & Cronin, K. (2012). Integrating social workers into medical-legal partnerships: Comprehensive problem solving for patients. *Social Work, 57*(4), 333–341. https://doi.org/10.1093/sw/sws012

Grapin, S. L., Collier-Meek, M. A., January, S. A., Yang, C., & Portillo, N. L. (2021). Reconceptualizing mentorship for the 21st century: A systematic mapping of research in school psychology. *School Psychology Review*. https://doi.org/10.1080/2372966X.2021.1910861

Haltaufderheide, J., Gather, J., Juckel, G., Schildmann, J., & Vollman, J. (2021). Types of ethical problems and expertise in clinical ethics consultation in psychiatry—insights from a qualitative empirical ethics study. *Frontiers in Psychiatry, 12*, 1–10. https://doi.org/10.3389/fpsyt.2021.558795

Jackson, S. (2021, June). *What is a cohort program?* Online Psychology Degree Guide. Retrieved January 14, 2022, from www.onlinepsychologydegree.info/faq/what-is-a-cohort-program

Lasser, J., & Klose, L. M. (2007). School psychologists' ethical decision making: Implications from selected social psychological phenomena. *School Psychology Review, 36*(3), 484–500.

Löfström, E., & Pyhältö, K. (2012). The supervisory relationship as an arena for ethical problem solving. *Education Research International, 2012*, 1–12. https://doi.org/10.1155/2012/961505

Peverly, S. T., Marcelin, G., & Kearn, M. (2014). Interventions for students with lecture note-taking difficulties. In J. T. Mascolo, V. C. Alfonso, & D. P. Flanagan (Eds.), *Essentials of planning, selecting, and tailoring interventions for unique learners* (pp. 387–414). Wiley.

Rasheem, S., Alleman, A., Mushonga, D., Anderson, D., & Vakalahi, H. F. (2018). Mentor-shape: Exploring the mentoring relationships of Black women in doctoral programs. *Mentoring & Tutoring: Partnership in Learning, 26*(1), 50–69. https://doi.org/10.1080/13611267.2018.1445443

Skinner, C. H., Pappas, D. N., & Davis, K. A. (2005). Enhancing academic engagement: Providing opportunities for responding and influencing students to choose to respond. *Psychology in the Schools, 42*(4), 389–403. https://doi.org/10.1002/pits.20065

Stenmark, C. K., Antes, A. L., Wang, X., Caughrom, J. J., Thiel, C. E., & Mumford, M. D. (2010). Strategies in forecasting outcomes in ethical decision-making: Identifying and analyzing the causes of the problem. *Ethics & Behavior, 20*(2), 110–127. https://doi.org/10.1080/10508421003595935

Svantesson, M., Löfmark, R., Thorsén, H., Kallenberg, K., & Ahlström, G. (2008). Learning a way through ethical problems: Swedish nurses' and doctors' experiences from one model of ethical rounds. *Journal of Medical Ethics, 34*(5), 399–406. https://doi.org/10.1136/jme.2006.019810

3 Ethical Decision-Making Models

Purpose and Use of Ethical Decision-Making Models

The purpose of using an ethical decision-making model is to carefully consider relevant ethical codes that may apply to the situation, weigh the different options of action and inaction and the resultant consequences of each, and to document your decision-making process (Jacob et al., 2022; Koocher & Keith-Spiegel, 1998). Particularly in contentious situations, which may not always be foreseen at the outset of the dilemma, it may be helpful to have documentation of the factors that were considered and how a decision was made in the moment. Many ethical texts within psychology and related fields, like applied behavior analysis, (e.g., Bailey & Burch, 2022; Drogin, 2019; Fisher, 2017; Jacob et al., 2022; Koocher & Keith-Spiegel, 2016; Sush & Najdowski, 2022), advocate for the use of an ethical decision-making model. In fact, the introduction of the NASP *Principles for Professional Ethics* (2020) states that a problem-solving process should be used when the practitioner is faced with difficult situations. Indeed, over a decade ago, Cottone (2012) expressed that psychologists who do not use an ethical decision-making model may present themselves as "naïve, uneducated, or potentially incompetent" (p. 117). This may be especially true for school psychologists, as the use of a decision-making model is represented in the NASP's *Best Practice in School Psychology* series (Klose & Lasser, 2014) and may be considered to be part of a school psychologist's standard of care.

Mitigating Decision-Making Factors

Despite the overwhelming support for the use of an ethical decision-making model by professional organizations and pillars within the psychological community, only 16% of school psychologists reported using a formal a decision-making model (Dailor & Jacob, 2011). Furthermore, there is a paucity of research supporting the notion that the use of a decision-making model improves the decision made by the practitioner (Boccio, 2021). In part, this may be because school psychologists often encounter ethical dilemmas where the decision-making process is influenced by factors beyond the facts of the situation. For example, Lasser et al. (2013) and Boccio et al. (2016) have expounded on situation specific factors that influence one's decision-making process, such as administrative pressures to make decisions that are not in the best interest of the most vulnerable individual (e.g., the student) and how Western ideology, or one's belief system, informs how we perceive dilemmas and their potential outcomes. A side-effect of these contextual pressures encountered by school psychologists are higher levels of burnout, lower levels of job satisfaction, and increased likelihood to leave the profession (Boccio et al., 2016).

DOI: 10.4324/9781003273950-3

Ethical Decision-Making Models

Several ethical decision-making models have been proposed in recent decades (Bailey & Burch, 2022; Boccio, 2021; Diamond et al., 2021; Drogin, 2019; Fischer, 2017; Williams et al., 2008). Possibly the most widely known model in school psychology is that of Koocher and Keith-Spiegel (1998), which delineated an eight-step model and was later adapted by Jacob et al. (2016). Given the amount of overlap among these models, the lack of empirical support demonstrating the enhancement of the ultimate decision made, and the lack of reported utilization among school psychologists, we will present and focus on the model created by Sush and Najdowski (2019). In particular, we gravitate toward the pragmatism and conciseness of this model. It is our assumption that some of the primary reasons practitioners do not employ a decision-making model more frequently are 1) they are unfamiliar with the models, 2) the models are too long to be easily remembered, and 3) the questions posed within the models are often perceived to be redundant. Our gravitation to the model promulgated by Sush and Najdowski is its brevity and visual simplicity that make it easy to recall, which may increase the likelihood it will be used in practice. Anecdotally, we have found in our own classrooms that graduate students completing Sush and Najdowski's workbook gained greater familiarity with the Behavior Analyst Certification Board's ethical code and an understanding of how to use an ethical decision-making model. By adopting this model for the NASP *Principles for Professional Ethics* (2020), we believe school psychologists and school psychology graduate students will receive the same benefits.

Sush and Najdowski's Model

As we mentioned before, a key benefit of the model created by Sush and Najdowski (2019) is its parsimony. Unlike many of the complex problem-solving models found in the psychology literature, this model utilizes only four steps, eliminating any repeat considerations across steps. In addition, we have infused aspects of an ethical decision-making model from a social justice perspective proposed by Diamond et al. (2021). We will describe these four steps as:

1. List all applicable ethics codes and standards.
2. Describe why those codes and standards apply to the current situation and whether a violation has occurred based on those codes and standards.
3. Identify contributing factors, including one's own belief system, and actions that could have been taken to avoid the scenario.
4. Select the ethical course of action moving forward, as well as risk factors and continued monitoring needs.

This model may be particularly useful for those following more than one ethical code, like many school psychologists do, as the first step deals with identifying which code(s) apply to the current situation. During this step, you will review each applicable ethical code and identify which standards in them apply to the scenario. While many students and practitioners may feel relatively confident in their memory of the ethical codes, we advise you to go directly to the documents so that the exact language of the code can be considered. Once you have a list of each code and standard that applies to the scenario, you are ready to move on to step two.

In step two, you will need to provide a rationale for why each code/standard applies to the scenario. Sometimes there will be an exact match between the scenario and standards, while other times the situation may be more complex and ambiguous. Carefully consider the factors within the scenario and how these factors are related to the ethical standards selected. We recommend the following questions when describing the rationale for considering the standards:

- Does the standard apply directly to the scenario? If so, how?
- Do multiple standards apply? Do these standards agree, or are they contradictory?

Once you have answered these questions, you will need to determine if an ethical violation has occurred. If a violation has not occurred, you can end the decision-making process here. If a violation has occurred, you would move to step three.

Step three asks you to identify antecedent conditions related to the scenario. Specifically, you should determine what factors may have led to the current scenario and how those factors could have been altered to prevent the scenario. Step three is a great time to use the assessment and problem-solving skills of a school psychologist to identify contributing variables. What had to happen for the current ethical scenario to take place? This is also an important time to attend to one's own belief system (e.g., learning history, bias, prejudice, culture, age, gender, ability, economic situation, etc.) and the impact it may be having on how the circumstances of the dilemma are perceived. Consider both directly related variables, as well as mitigating factors like the ones discussed previously in this chapter. Then, identify ways in which those variables could have been changed to prevent the current situation.

Once the relevant codes and standards have been determined and contributing factors have been identified, it is time to decide on a course of action. In the particular situation of the dilemma, ask yourself what needs to happen to rectify the ethical violation. Depending on the magnitude and severity of the violation, the course of action can take several paths. If you become aware of someone else's ethical violation, general recommendations are to first discuss the violation with the person involved so that they can rectify the situation themselves. In cases where they do not rectify the situation, or when the violation is severe, you may need to report the violation to the appropriate organizations and licensing boards, supervisors, and potentially law enforcement (APA, 2017). When you are directly involved in the ethical dilemma, make a plan for responding to the current situation, and make a plan to avoid future instances of this situation. When making this plan, consider risk factors. What contributing factors led to the current situation, and do these factors remain relevant or of concern? Are you able to change these factors, or will you need to work with others to try to prevent them from occurring in the future? How will you monitor these factors and others to ensure ethical violations can be prevented prior to their occurrence? In the next section, we will walk you through some example case scenarios using the decision-making model and materials provided in this book.

Using this Book

Each subsequent chapter of this book will provide a description of ethical standards in the NASP *Principles for Professional Ethics* (NASP, 2020), as well as practice case scenarios related to these standards. The scenarios will range from simple to complex. While this text will focus on the NASP *Principles for Professional Ethics*, some scenarios may indicate multiple licensing boards or organizations involved in the situation. These additional factors were included for doctoral, or dual-program, graduate students who are likely to be learning about other ethical codes and for practitioners who possess multiple credentials and organizational memberships that require them to adhere to additional ethical codes. In these cases, it may be necessary to consult multiple ethical codes. The scenarios will be presented in workbook pages, where you will move through the steps of the ethical decision-making model described previously. In this section, we will show you a completed example, while the worksheets in the chapters will be blank for your use.

In addition to completing the scenarios using the ethical decision-making model, we also encourage you to practice consulting with others regarding these cases. If you are completing these scenarios as part of a graduate class, consult with your classmates, peer mentor, and field-based supervisor. If you are a practitioner, we encourage you to consult with your colleagues. Practitioners may even consider creating a book club to build community, further professional development, and as a way to mentor less experienced practitioners. Consultation and collaboration with others are skills related to all aspects of school psychology practice and comprise Domain 2 within the NASP Practice Model (NASP, 2020).

It is important to begin practicing consultation early in one's career (i.e., as a graduate student). Although it may seem like you will never see or interact with the people in your graduate program again, it is likely that your relationships will extend well beyond graduate school. Graduates often gain employment from school districts within the same state as the program they attended and subsequently will see each other at professional development opportunities over the years and at their state's school psychology professional conference. In our experience, over time, conferences and conventions become just as much about gaining professional development as they do about catching up with long-time friends. It has also been our experience, and observation, that graduates are sometimes even employed by the same district and work alongside each other, again, highlighting the benefit of establishing strong working, collaborative, relationships early during graduate school. School psychology is a relatively small field, and even if we do not work within the same school district, we are likely to see each other's reports as students transfer between districts. Therefore, we highly encourage you to use this time and these opportunities to practice your consultation skills. Everyone has a unique background, culture, learning history, and belief system that influences their frame of reference. By sharing your perspectives, you enhance your own professional growth as your viewpoint can be challenged and honed and the perspectives of those you consult with benefit from the exposure to a different way of analyzing the case.

Diversity

Previously in this chapter, we introduced an ethical decision-making model and the importance of collaboration in ethical problem-solving process. Our recommendations to use both a decision-making model and collaboration are meant to remove some level of subjectivity from the decision-making process, or at least for that subjectivity to have been considered and agreed on by multiple parties. Within the area of subjectivity, we must also discuss the impact of diversity on ethical decision-making. The field of school psychology is dominated by White, middle-aged, monolingual females (Walcott & Hyson, 2018). In fact, 88% of NASP members reported being White and 83% reported being female. Similarly, most teachers are middle-age White females. According to a recent report based on a representative sample of teachers and principals in 2017–2018, 79% of public school teachers reported being non-Hispanic White, 77% reported being female, and the mean age was 43 years (Institute of Educational Sciences, 2020). The sex and racial composition of school psychologists and teachers working in schools is in contrast to those they serve. The Institute of Educational Sciences (2021) reported that in the Fall of 2018 only 47% of public school students reported being White. This is a decrease from a reported 54% of White students in the Fall of 2009. Furthermore, during the 2017–2018 school year, 51.4% of public school students were reported to be male (Civil Rights Data Collection, 2021).

Recognizing the stark contrast between the field of school psychology and the students we serve, the NASP African American subcommittee of the Multicultural Affairs Committee created the NASP Exposure Project (NASP, 2022). The purpose of the NASP Exposure Project is to inform high school students and undergraduate students of the field of school psychology. In part, it is hoped that bringing increased awareness to the field will reduce the critical shortage in school psychology and create a more culturally and linguistically diverse workforce that is more representative of those we serve. Interested readers are encouraged to learn more by visiting the NASP website at www.nasponline.org/resources-and-publications/resources-and-podcasts/diversity-and-social-justice/cultural-competence/multicultural-affairs-committee/nasp-exposure-project-(nasp-ep) and by listening to Dr. Charles Barrett discuss the initiative on the Texas Association of School Psychologists (TASP) Talks Podcast at https://podcasts.apple.com/us/podcast/ep-19-fall-convention-preview-with-dr-charles-barrett/id1570910285?i=1000538422014. By becoming more representative, the field is more likely to provide more culturally responsive and competent services that, in turn, result in greater treatment fidelity and efficacy. However, it should be made clear that it is not the responsibility of marginalized individuals to enhance the service provision of the field. That responsibility lies with each of us in the profession. For that reason, you will notice some intentional decisions in this text to help you consider diverse perspectives, or expose you to issues that are not likely representative of your experiences.

Case Scenarios

The names used in the case scenarios were purposefully made diverse. This is not to covertly or overtly imply that marginalized individuals disproportionately engage in unethical practices. Instead, the diversity of names was selected to present our hope for a near future in which school psychology is represented by a diverse workforce.

Case scenarios were created from our imaginations based on our collective experiences working in public schools, charter schools, private practice, and clinics; experiences of personal friends that are school psychologists; supervising practicum and intern students; mentoring students and early career professionals; experiences of other school psychologists that share their stories in online forums; and news reports. Although case scenarios are based in reality, no scenario represents an actual event, school or clinic, or individual. While some cases may appear more unbelievable than others, they are all inspired by true events.

The creation of the case scenarios was shaped by our own experiences and belief systems. It is probable our own biases have manifested themselves in the scenarios, as well as in the sample problem-solving steps we have provided. This is yet another reason why we encourage readers to engage in collaborative consultation with others, even if you initially complete the scenarios privately. Everyone has a unique background and learning history that shapes their belief system and approach to resolving ethical dilemmas. By having an open and critical discussion about one's perspective on the events depicted and how one arrived at the conclusions they did, others are likely to learn from them. In addition, it allows others to respectfully challenge one's thought processes and reasoning for making the decision, or more likely assumptions that led to the proposed decision. By being open to engaging in these types of discussions, the more likely biases and blind spots will be identified, which will allow for personal and professional growth to occur. Blind spots are so called because we are, in fact, blind to them. One way to identify blind spots is for other people to help us recognize their presence and for us to be in a position to accept the feedback, recognize it, and take action to address it. Another potential way to identify blind spots is to seek professional development in areas we may not be naturally inclined to attend, either because we do not have interest in the topic or because we believe the topic is something that is not an issue for us personally (e.g., microaggressions).

Case scenarios were also written based on the Publication Manual of the American Psychological Association's guidelines for bias-free language (American Psychological Association, 2020). At times, purposeful deviation from bias-free language was used to represent an ethical dilemma within the case scenario. Users of this book are encouraged to explore within their ethical decision-making model responses and discussions with colleagues, the language that is used within the case studies, and the biases or assumptions it may provoke within themselves. For example, a person's name alone may invoke certain assumptions about the individual if it is the same as a person famous for certain actions commonly looked down upon by large segments of society or if the name is closely linked to a historical figure and/or individual represented in religious texts.

Application

The following sample case scenario is provided to give you a framework for completing the rest of the case scenarios contained in the book. After reading the scenario, we recommend you complete the provided ethical problem-solving model on your own before comparing your responses with your peers and ours. Given everyone's unique background, experiences, and belief system, it is likely that there will be some variation in responses based on individuals' backgrounds, experiences, and belief systems. Presenting an ethical dilemma within a brief paragraph presents challenges as much of the context or nuance of the situation cannot be included. However, this highlights the importance of collaborative consultation with others all the more. Engage in respectful discussion with your peers about these variations and why they occurred. Carefully examine what it was about the scenario that led you to differing assumptions. Readers may also consider reading *Crucial Conversations: Tools for Talking When Stakes Are High* (Grenny et al., 2022) and *Race Talk and the Conspiracy of Silence: Understanding and Facilitating Difficult Dialogues on Race* (Sue, 2015) to help facilitate productive conversations.

Sample Scenario

Ms. Castillo, a school psychologist, has recently lost her husband to a terminal illness. She is experiencing extreme grief and is having difficulty with perspective taking. While she feels a longer absence from her job may be warranted, Ms. Castillo goes back to work because of the lack of other service providers and encouragement from others to "get back to normal" as soon as possible. During a counseling session with a student who has a history of depression, Ms. Castillo tells the student that their problems are small, and they should be grateful they do not have any real problems. Ms. Castillo is a Nationally Certified School Psychologist and a member of APA.

Table 3.1

Step 1: List all applicable ethics codes and standards.	NASP: II.1.2 Personal Problems APA: 2.06. Personal Problems and Conflicts
Step 2: Describe why those codes and standards apply to the current situation and whether a violation has occurred based on those codes and standards.	The above standards in the NASP and APA codes apply to this scenario directly. Ms. Castillo is experiencing extreme grief and difficulty with perspective taking, which has influenced her ability to perform her duties with competence and care for her clients. The standards identified are in alignment with this scenario. Based on the scenario and the related codes, an ethical violation has occurred.

Step 3: Identify contributing factors, including one's own belief system, and actions that could have been taken to avoid the scenario.	The primary contributing factors are Ms. Castillo's personal experiences. Her husband's death, the direct contributing factor, could not have been prevented in this scenario. Mitigating factors may include the lack other qualified service providers and encouragement from others to "get back to normal" too quickly, and a personal belief that helping others is more important than attending to her own needs. Mitigating factors could have been avoided if she were not the sole service provider in her schools and if others had allowed her the time she needed to mourn prior to engaging in-service provision. Additionally, Ms. Castillo's difficulty with perspective taking and her life experiences may have prevented her from being firm in her need for additional time prior to beginning service provision, or in her response to the client.
Step 4: Select the ethical course of action moving forward, as well as risk factors and continued monitoring needs.	Attempting an informal resolution may be appropriate as a first step. The chosen course of action in this situation is to: • Discuss the situation with Ms. Castillo. Encourage her to meet with the client to repair the relationship, and then to consider steps to take to prevent future violations, such as taking additional time off work, or asking a trusted colleague to monitor/supervise her until she is feeling better able to provide services independently. • If Ms. Castillo does not choose to follow-through with rectifying the situation, the supervisor will be consulted. It is also possible, depending on Ms. Castillo's response and risk of repeat violations, that the violation is reported to NASP, APA, and the state credentialing board. Risk factors in this situation include Ms. Castillo's ongoing grief, lack of other qualified service providers, and personal beliefs about others being more important than she is. Recommendations will be made for additional time off and/or temporary consultation or supervision for Ms. Castillo. Additional recommendations will include recruiting additional service providers, either full-time, or contracting as needed, for times when the primary service provider is unable to maintain duties. Ms. Castillo may also consider working with a counselor regarding work-life balance and setting boundaries so that her needs are met. Monitoring will need to take place if Ms. Castillo will continue providing psychological services following resolution of this ethical violation. In this event, a consultant or supervisor may be temporarily assigned to monitor Ms. Castillo's ethical and competent completion of services.

Summary

Ultimately, the ethical decision-making model used in this book will guide you through identifying the relevant ethical codes and standards for a scenario, describing how and why those codes and standards apply and whether, based on them, an ethical violation has occurred. It will also help you identify factors that contributed to the scenario, as well as to make a plan to remedy the violation and put steps in place to monitor and prevent similar scenarios in the future. Similar to a behavioral problem-solving model, these steps first require you to identify and validate the problem, then identify the function, or cause, of the problem, and finally develop an intervention or behavior change plan.

Reference List

American Psychological Association. (2017, January 1). *Ethical principles of psychologists and code of conduct.* www.apa.org/ethics/code/ethics-code-2017.pdf

American Psychological Association. (2020). *Publication manual of the American Psychological Association* (7th ed.). American Psychological Association.

Bailey, J. S., & Burch, M. R. (2022). *Ethics for behavior analysts* (4th ed.). Routledge.

Boccio, D. E. (2021). Does use of a decision-making model improve the quality of school psychologists' ethical decisions? *Ethics & Behavior, 31*(2), 119–235. https://doi.org/10.1080/10508422.2020.1715802

Boccio, D. E., Weisz, G., & Lefkowitz, R. (2016). Administrative pressure to practice unethically and burnout within the profession of school psychology. *Psychology in the Schools, 53*(6), 659–672. https://doi.org/10.1002/pits.21931

Canadian Psychological Association. (2017, January 1). *Canadian code of ethics for psychologists* (4th ed.). https://cpa.ca/docs/File/Ethics/CPA_Code_2017_4thEd.pdf

Chalk, R., Frankel, M. S., & Chafer, S. B. (1980). *AAAS professional ethics project.* American Association for the Advancement of Science.

Civil Rights Data Collection. (2021, June). *An overview of exclusionary discipline practices in public school for the 2017–2018 school year.* Retrieved January 6, 2022, from https://www2.ed.gov/about/offices/list/ocr/docs/crdc-exclusionary-school-discipline.pdf

Cottone, R. R. (2012). Ethical decision making in mental health contexts: Representative models and an organizational framework. In S. J. Knapp, M. C. Gottlieb, M. M. Handelsman, & L. D. VandeCreek (Eds.), *APA handbook of ethics in psychology* (Vol. 1, pp. 99–122). American Psychological Association. https://doi.org/10.1037/13271-004

Dailor, A. N., & Jacob, S. (2011). Ethically challenging situations reported by school psychologists: Implications for training. *Psychology in the Schools, 48*(6), 619–631. https://doi.org/10.1002/pits.v48.6

Diamond, E., Whalen, A., Kelly, K. K., & Davis, S. (2021, June). DECIDE: An ethical decision-making model supporting a socially just practice. *Communique, 49*(8), 4–7. www.nasponline.org/x28229.xml

Drogin, E. Y. (2019). *Ethical conflicts in psychology* (5th ed.). American Psychological Association.

Fisher, C. B. (2017). *Decoding the ethics code: A practical guide for psychologists* (4th ed.). Sage.

Grenny, J., Patterson, K., McMillan, R., Switzler, A., & Gregory, E. (2022). *Crucial conversations: Tools for talking when stakes are high* (3rd ed.). McGraw Hill.

Institute of Educational Sciences. (2020, April). *Characteristics of public and private elementary and secondary school teachers in the United States: Results from the 2017–2018 national teacher and principal survey.* Retrieved January 6, 2022, from https://nces.ed.gov/pubs2020/2020142.pdf

Institute of Educational Sciences. (2021, May). *Racial/ethnic enrollment in public schools.* Retrieved January 6, 2022, from https://nces.ed.gov/programs/coe/indicator/cge

International School Psychology Association. (2021). *Code of ethics.* www.ispaweb.org/wp-content/uploads/2020/07/The_ISPA_Code_of_Ethics_2011.pdf

Jacob, S. (2014). Best practices in ethical school psychological practice. In P. L. Harrison & A. Thomas (Eds.), *Best practices in school psychology: Foundations* (pp. 437–448). NASP.

Jacob, S., Decker, D. M., & Lugg, E. T. (2016). *Ethics and law for school psychologists* (7th ed.). John Wiley & Sons, Inc.

Jacob, S., Decker, D. M., Lugg, E. T., & Diamond, E. (2022). *Ethics and law for school psychologists* (8th ed.). John Wiley & Sons, Inc.

Klose, L. M., & Lasser, J. (2014). Best practices in the application of professional ethics. In P. L. Harrison & A. Thomas (Eds.), *Best practices in school psychology: Foundations* (pp. 449–458). NASP.

Koocher, G. P., & Keith-Spiegel, P. (1998). *Ethics in psychology: Professional standards and cases.* Oxford University Press.

Koocher, G. P., & Keith-Spiegel, P. (2016). *Ethics in psychology and the mental health professions: Standards and cases* (4th ed.). Oxford University Press.

Lasser, J., Klose, L. M., & Robillard, R. (2013). Context-sensitive ethics in school psychology. *Contemporary School Psychology, 17*(1), 119–128. https://doi.org/10.1007/BF03340993

National Association of School Psychologists. (2020). *The professional standards of the National Association of School Psychologists.* Retrieved May 1, 2021, from www.nasponline.org/x55315.xml

National Association of School Psychologists. (2022). *NASP exposure project (NASP-EP).* Retrieved January 6, 2022, from www.nasponline.org/resources-and-publications/resources-and-podcasts/diversity-and-social-justice/cultural-competence/multicultural-affairs-committee/nasp-exposure-project-(nasp-ep)

Sue, D. W. (2015). *Race talk and the conspiracy of silence: Understanding and facilitating difficult dialogues on race.* Wiley.

Sush, D. J., & Najdowski, A. C. (2019). *A workbook of ethical case scenarios in applied behavior analysis.* Academic Press.

Sush, D. J., & Najdowski, A. C. (2022). *A workbook of ethical case scenarios in applied behavior analysis* (2nd ed.). Academic Press.

Walcott, C. M., & Hyson, D. (2018). *Results from the NASP 2015 membership survey, part one: Demographics and employment conditions* [Research report]. National Association of School Psychologists.

Williams, B. B., Armistead, L., & Jacob, S. (2008). *Professional ethics for school psychologists: A problem-solving model casebook.* National Association of School Psychologists.

4 Scenarios for Consent and Assent

Introduction

Issues of autonomy and self-determination are foundational to ethical standards across caregiving professions. When it comes to providing psychological services, it is important to recognize individuals' right to contribute to and consent to services. While the issue of consent may seem straightforward, in the section that follows we will describe several situations in which consent is and is not required, many of which may not be intuitive. When in doubt about whether consent or assent is required, we encourage you to check with your relevant ethical codes.

Guiding Principle I.1 Autonomy and Self-Determination

Guiding Principle I.1 Autonomy and Self-Determination (NASP, 2020) pertains to consent, assent, and the right to refuse or revoke consent. Issues of when consent is and is not needed to provide service or to disclose information are interwoven throughout every aspect of school psychologists' work. The standards within this Guiding Principle provide practitioners with the information needed to make informed decisions regarding their practice. In particular, practicum students, interns, and trainees will want to attend to Standard I.1.3 Seeking Informed Consent (NASP, 2020), as they are specifically mentioned within this standard.

The issue of when consent is or is not required may not always be readily identified. In general, consent for consultation is not required if the implementation of the intervention does not require the oversight or skill set of the school psychologist. In other words, the intervention must be under the purview of someone else (e.g., teacher, support team) and be part of the normal classroom routine. School psychologists may also provide input that is focused on class-wide issues and review individual school records for purposes related to their assigned duties without first obtaining informed consent. If school psychologists are part of district or campus-wide screenings, such as when gathering benchmark data or conducting universal screeners, they also do not need to obtain informed parental consent. However, in general, consent is required when the intervention is directed by the school psychologist, pertains to an individual student, or encroaches on the privacy of the family to an undue degree. When universal screeners gather data about mental health problems, parents must be given notice and be allowed to withdraw their consent for their child to participate. Graduate students and practitioners are also encouraged to consult with their local and state laws and policies regarding the issue of when to obtain consent. For example, in 2012, the Texas State Board of Examiners of Psychologists (TSBEP), who credential school psychologists as Licensed Specialists in School Psychology (LSSP), published additional guidance to its

DOI: 10.4324/9781003273950-4

licensees regarding this issue given the confusion many LSSPs were experiencing at the time (TSBEP, 2012).

If a student presents as a risk to oneself or others, or is in danger from others, school psychologists may also provide services without notice or consent. Assistance may be provided to those students who self-refer on a one-time basis, or if more information is needed to determine the severity of the situation, school psychologists may provide services until the severity is determined. If permissible by your specific state and by district policy, then services may also be provided to mature minors without consent. If this is not the case in your state or district, then consent is both ethically and legally required.

When informed consent is needed, school psychologists must work to make sure the individual providing consent is truly informed as to what they are consenting to. Standard I.1.3 Seeking Informed Consent (NASP, 2020) provides a list of items that must be discussed when seeking informed consent. While we will not re-present that list here, we do want to highlight a few aspects of informed consent. For example, when seeking informed consent, practitioners must attend to linguistic and cultural factors and provide the information in language that is developmentally appropriate to the audience. Further, consent must be received in writing. As the old adage goes, if it is not in writing, it did not happen. One of the unheralded duties of school psychologists is making sure documentation exists for services rendered. In addition, informed consent should be obtained before practicum students or interns begin providing services. When services are provided by practicum students and interns, the supervisory relationship must be explained, and their supervisor identified, so parents or guardians know who to contact if they have any questions or concerns. When parent(s) or guardian(s) refuse or revoke informed consent, school psychologists must honor this and not engage in retribution. Instead, school psychologists should offer alternate recommendations that may be more palatable. When approval for services is sought from a minor, the term assent is used instead of consent. Seeking assent respects the dignity and welfare of the minor by ensuring they understand what they are being asked to agree to, using developmentally appropriate communication, and honoring their refusal to, or withdrawal of, assent. However, seeking assent may not always be appropriate. When this is the case, carefully explain to the minor instances when you cannot honor the minor's refusal to assent. One way this may come up in practice is when you have received informed consent to complete a psychoeducational evaluation. In this case, you would not be able to honor the student's refusal for assent. Instead, you should explain the process and rational for the activities you will be doing together and how the information will be used. Aside from the ethical implications, refusing to respect one's lack of assent after seeking it may damage your ability to establish rapport with the student. So, while true assent may not always be able to be obtained or honored, the process of informing the student of their role in the process, and the process itself, should occur.

Let's Practice

Below are a set of case scenarios to help you familiarize yourself with potential ethical dilemmas in the areas of consent and assent as a school psychologist. We recommend completing the scenario worksheets individually and then collaboratively in pairs or groups in order to hear multiple perspectives. As you might notice when reviewing the scenarios, it is possible to come to a different conclusion or consider alternative factors than others. This is why these situations are called ethical *dilemmas*. When working collaboratively, there is opportunity for sharing different perspectives, which may ultimately lead to better problem-solving. Chapter 3 provides an overview of the ethical decision-making model and a guide to using the worksheets that follow.

Reference List

National Association of School Psychologists. (2020). *The professional standards of the National Association of School Psychologists.* Retrieved May 1, 2021, from www.nasponline.org/x55315.xml

Texas State Board of Examiners of Psychologists. (2012). Analysis of impact of federal education law on board rules governing informed consent. *TSBEP Newsletter.* https://tasp.memberclicks.net/assets/conference-materials/2016/ethics%20for%20lssps%20-%20informed%20consent%20tsbep%20-%20donna%20black%20-%20tasp%202013.pdf

Practice Scenarios

Scenario 1

During the afternoon, Ms. Adams, a fourth-grade teacher at Sunset Elementary, calls your office telephone. She has a student who will not leave the bathroom and is crying following recess. You walk to the bathroom, where the identified student is washing their hands but is still crying and refusing to return to class. You identify this as an emergency situation, given the intensity of crying behavior and class refusal and decide to engage the student in psychological services. You introduce yourself as the school psychologist and ask if they want to talk to you about why they are upset. The student agrees, and you go to your office, where you engage in rapport-building and motivational interviewing techniques. Through this information gathering, you learn the student's friends are mad at them, and that they feel they did not do anything wrong and do not understand why the friends are upset. While this does not seem like an emergency anymore, you complete your session with the student, and send them to class when they are feeling better. Given that it seems the problem is solved, the student's parents are not notified of the incident or of their child's meeting with you.

Step 1: List all applicable ethics codes and standards.	
Step 2: Describe why those codes and standards apply to the current situation and whether a violation has occurred based on those codes and standards.	
Step 3: Identify contributing factors, including one's own belief system, and actions that could have been taken to avoid the scenario.	
Step 4: Select the ethical course of action moving forward, as well as risk factors and continued monitoring needs.	

Scenario 2

At the beginning of the school year Mr. Roark met with the parents of Dawid to obtain informed consent for a psychoeducational evaluation to assist in determining if Dawid meets criteria for special education services. At the meeting, Mr. Roark carefully explained the nature and scope of services he would be providing, went over the foreseeable benefits, risks, and costs with the parents; discussed limits of confidentiality; who will be able to access information from the evaluation; and the possible consequences of consenting to the evaluation. The explanations were given in the parents' native language and in a manner that was consistent with their culture and understandable to the parents. Unfortunately, Mr. Roark contracted COVID-19 shortly after obtaining consent and is now very concerned about completing the evaluation within the designated timeline. In order to meet the deadline, Mr. Roark instructs the intern he supervises to complete the cognitive and achievement evaluations. Mr. Roark will still write the report and attend the meeting to provide a comprehensible explanation to the parents.

Step 1: List all applicable ethics codes and standards.	
Step 2: Describe why those codes and standards apply to the current situation and whether a violation has occurred based on those codes and standards.	
Step 3: Identify contributing factors, including one's own belief system, and actions that could have been taken to avoid the scenario.	
Step 4: Select the ethical course of action moving forward, as well as risk factors and continued monitoring needs.	

Scenario 3

Mrs. Conlon, school psychologist of Milton Middle School, has had a long and tumultuous relationship with the Huffman family. Most recently, Mr. and Mrs. Huffman called to revoke special education services for their youngest son, Brian, who is currently receiving services for Other Health Impairment. Mrs. Conlon was quite disturbed and upset at this news because Brian's behavior has become increasingly erratic and violent. Before hanging up with the parents Mrs. Conlon informed the parents she would give them two weeks to reconsider their decision and if they did not allow services to continue she would have to expel Brian from the school.

Step 1: List all applicable ethics codes and standards.	
Step 2: Describe why those codes and standards apply to the current situation and whether a violation has occurred based on those codes and standards.	
Step 3: Identify contributing factors, including one's own belief system, and actions that could have been taken to avoid the scenario.	
Step 4: Select the ethical course of action moving forward, as well as risk factors and continued monitoring needs.	

Scenario 4

A school psychology intern, Jia Yi, recently attended a didactic training on informed consent and assent. During the training she realizes she had not been seeking assent from the students she works with and vows to never make this mistake again. The following day when she goes to retrieve a student to administer a cognitive assessment, as part of an evaluation to determine emotional disturbance, she seeks assent from Crystal, the student. Crystal quickly becomes agitated and begins yelling at Jia Yi that she does not assent. Saddened at this result, but not wanting her supervisor's credential to be jeopardized or her future ability to become a school psychologist, she honors the student's refusal to assent and discontinues attempts to complete the evaluation. At the Individualized Education Program (IEP) meeting she informs the team she was not able to complete the evaluation because assent was not obtained.

Step 1: List all applicable ethics codes and standards.	
Step 2: Describe why those codes and standards apply to the current situation and whether a violation has occurred based on those codes and standards.	
Step 3: Identify contributing factors, including one's own belief system, and actions that could have been taken to avoid the scenario.	
Step 4: Select the ethical course of action moving forward, as well as risk factors and continued monitoring needs.	

Scenario 5

Jorge has been directed to consult with a fifth-grade teacher, Mrs. Hellenschmidt, who is having difficulties with one of her students, Michael. Mrs. Hellenschmidt describes Michael as being off task all the time every day and very disruptive to the classroom. When asked to define "disruptive" she explains that Michael often makes jokes, causing the other students to laugh. Michael also frequently blurts out answers and roams the classroom. After understanding the topography of the behavior, Jorge recommends Mrs. Hellenschmidt use a token economy to address Michael's behavior. Jorge has to explain how token economies work, write up a plan, and prepare the materials for Mrs. Hellenschmidt to implement because she has never used a token economy before. He then returns on Monday to explain the behavioral expectations to Michael and ensure Mrs. Hellenschmidt implements the plan with fidelity.

Step 1: List all applicable ethics codes and standards.	
Step 2: Describe why those codes and standards apply to the current situation and whether a violation has occurred based on those codes and standards.	
Step 3: Identify contributing factors, including one's own belief system, and actions that could have been taken to avoid the scenario.	
Step 4: Select the ethical course of action moving forward, as well as risk factors and continued monitoring needs.	

Scenario 6

Clark Esar recently moved to a new state and started a job as a school psychologist after practicing in another state for the past ten years. Quintin, a tenth-grade student, requests counseling services from Mr. Esar. They report feelings of intense anxiety throughout the day and have a diagnosis of Generalized Anxiety Disorder, given by their primary care physician, and take a daily medication to treat anxiety. The student does not receive any special education services or accommodations at school. In your previous state, mature minors could request and receive school psychological services without parental consent. Given Quintin is 16 years old, you determine they are mature enough to seek services without parental consent and agree to provide counseling services. After six weeks of providing counseling services to Quintin, you receive an angry call from Quintin's father. He is upset that he was not notified of the services and did not consent to them. You learn through this phone call that your current state law does not allow you to provide psychological services to mature minors without parental consent.

Step 1: List all applicable ethics codes and standards.	
Step 2: Describe why those codes and standards apply to the current situation and whether a violation has occurred based on those codes and standards.	
Step 3: Identify contributing factors, including one's own belief system, and actions that could have been taken to avoid the scenario.	
Step 4: Select the ethical course of action moving forward, as well as risk factors and continued monitoring needs.	

Scenario 7

A kindergarten student is referred by the student referral team for an evaluation to determine eligibility for special education services, with several concerns about developmental delays expressed. The parents agree and provide consent for the evaluation, and the school psychologist, Dr. Davy Lofting, begins the evaluation process. After completing testing and writing his evaluation report the parents contact Dr. Lofting. They wish to stop the evaluation, as they do not want their student to be labeled and receive special education services at school. They would prefer to speak to their pediatrician about possibilities for diagnoses and services outside of the school setting. Dr. Lofting steers the parents away from seeking external help, telling them that the professionals at school know best what services would be right for their child. The parents ultimately concede and agree for Dr. Lofting to complete the report and for the team to determine special education eligibility.

Step 1: List all applicable ethics codes and standards.	
Step 2: Describe why those codes and standards apply to the current situation and whether a violation has occurred based on those codes and standards.	
Step 3: Identify contributing factors, including one's own belief system, and actions that could have been taken to avoid the scenario.	
Step 4: Select the ethical course of action moving forward, as well as risk factors and continued monitoring needs.	

Scenario 8

Mr. Hines, a second-grade teacher at Sunrise Elementary, requests to consult with you about his classroom management. Mr. Hines has noticed that several of his students talk out and leave their assigned seats during instruction and would like to modify his class-wide behavior management strategies to address these behaviors. While you are observing Mr. Hines' class, you notice one student appears to be the instigator of these behaviors. During instruction, this student is usually the first to talk out or leave their seat, then other students follow their lead. When you develop the class-wide behavior management plan with Mr. Hines, you suggest a group contingency, where rewards for the class are contingent on the identified student's behavior. No consent is collected from any student's parents or guardians. The identified student tells their parents about the new classroom intervention, and their mother calls the school. She is upset that her student has been singled out, and that she was never notified of the intervention or of her student's difficulties in the classroom.

Step 1: List all applicable ethics codes and standards.	
Step 2: Describe why those codes and standards apply to the current situation and whether a violation has occurred based on those codes and standards.	
Step 3: Identify contributing factors, including one's own belief system, and actions that could have been taken to avoid the scenario.	
Step 4: Select the ethical course of action moving forward, as well as risk factors and continued monitoring needs.	

Scenario 9

The principal of Lincoln High calls the school psychologist, Ms. Shiff, to ask for assistance with one of their students, Julia, who was found cutting her arms in the gym locker room. Ms. Shiff politely informs the principal he will need to get informed consent from Julia's parents before she can intervene and provide psychological assistance or assess the situation.

Step 1: List all applicable ethics codes and standards.	
Step 2: Describe why those codes and standards apply to the current situation and whether a violation has occurred based on those codes and standards.	
Step 3: Identify contributing factors, including one's own belief system, and actions that could have been taken to avoid the scenario.	
Step 4: Select the ethical course of action moving forward, as well as risk factors and continued monitoring needs.	

Scenario 10

You are in your sixth year as a school psychologist and have agreed to supervise a practicum student. The practicum student has a set of course requirements they have to complete, such as a complete psychoeducational evaluation and behavioral consultation cases, and you have them complete other items, as well. As part of your supervision of the practicum student, you have them administer tests of cognitive abilities as part of a student's psychoeducational evaluation while you observe. You plan to provide feedback to the practicum student and determine if they are ready to complete an evaluation independently based on your observation. Since you were in the room during all parts of the assessment, and the practicum student falls under your certification, you did not notify the child's parents that the practicum student may administer some or all of the tests. The parents learn that the practicum student administered some tests and are upset they were not notified. They deem these results to be invalid and request the school fund an independent educational evaluation.

Step 1: List all applicable ethics codes and standards.	
Step 2: Describe why those codes and standards apply to the current situation and whether a violation has occurred based on those codes and standards.	
Step 3: Identify contributing factors, including one's own belief system, and actions that could have been taken to avoid the scenario.	
Step 4: Select the ethical course of action moving forward, as well as risk factors and continued monitoring needs.	

Scenario 11

Two weeks ago, Winston, a 14-year-old male, told the school psychologist, Dr. Agger, that he is gay, but is scared that his friends and his family will not accept him if they find out. In particular, he is afraid his mother will disown him and kick him out of the house. Dr. Agger has been meeting with Winston to discuss the situation and help him find support within the community. At their last meeting, Winston requested an evaluation for special education services because he thinks he might have a learning disability and Attention Deficit/Hyperactivity Disorder. However, Winston does not want Dr. Agger to get consent from his parents because he is afraid they will find out he has been seeing the school psychologist and request the notes Dr. Agger has been taking during their meetings together and find out that he is gay.

Step 1: List all applicable ethics codes and standards.	
Step 2: Describe why those codes and standards apply to the current situation and whether a violation has occurred based on those codes and standards.	
Step 3: Identify contributing factors, including one's own belief system, and actions that could have been taken to avoid the scenario.	
Step 4: Select the ethical course of action moving forward, as well as risk factors and continued monitoring needs.	

Scenario 12

Ms. Morris, NCSP received consent from both parents of a fifth-grade student for a psychoeducational evaluation. Two weeks later, after already completing the ADOS-2, UNIT-2, CARS-2, and direct observations, the parents revoke consent for evaluation. Ms. Morris informs the parents that it is too late to revoke consent because she has already nearly completed the evaluation and offers them a few dates and times to meet with the IEP team to determine eligibility for services.

Step 1: List all applicable ethics codes and standards.	
Step 2: Describe why those codes and standards apply to the current situation and whether a violation has occurred based on those codes and standards.	
Step 3: Identify contributing factors, including one's own belief system, and actions that could have been taken to avoid the scenario.	
Step 4: Select the ethical course of action moving forward, as well as risk factors and continued monitoring needs.	

Scenario 13

Dr. Barbara Johnson has been providing psychoeducational assessment through a private practice after school hours and sometimes on the weekends. Last Friday around 5:30 pm a client of one of the other providers in the practice walked in with blood running down his wrists and looking pale. When Dr. Johnson inquired what had happened the client said that his dads had just told him they were getting a divorce so he had cut his own wrists in the parking lot. Dr. Johnson informs the individual that his therapist is not in and that he will need to sign an informed consent with her in order to talk about what is going on.

Step 1: List all applicable ethics codes and standards.	
Step 2: Describe why those codes and standards apply to the current situation and whether a violation has occurred based on those codes and standards.	
Step 3: Identify contributing factors, including one's own belief system, and actions that could have been taken to avoid the scenario.	
Step 4: Select the ethical course of action moving forward, as well as risk factors and continued monitoring needs.	

Scenario 14

Dr. Sue is a licensed psychologist, board certified behavior analyst, and nationally certified school psychologist. He has been seeing Lightner, a 12-year-old boy, in his private practice for reading issues for the past seven months. Lightner's mother, Mrs. McKay, informed Dr. Sue that she and Lightner's teachers have seen no improvement in his reading abilities and as such, she will not be bringing her son for any more sessions. Instead, she will be seeking services from other providers. Dr. Sue tells Mrs. McKay she should not do this, that Lightner is on the verge of a major breakthrough in reading and that she needs to be patient. He also warns her that if she refuses to continue receiving services from him prematurely that he will warn the other practitioners in the area not to work with her or her son.

Step 1: List all applicable ethics codes and standards.	
Step 2: Describe why those codes and standards apply to the current situation and whether a violation has occurred based on those codes and standards.	
Step 3: Identify contributing factors, including one's own belief system, and actions that could have been taken to avoid the scenario.	
Step 4: Select the ethical course of action moving forward, as well as risk factors and continued monitoring needs.	

Scenario 15

Joanna Hamm has been working as a school psychologist at the Unified School District of the Palms and has been a member of the crisis response team for the past two months. She has never been allowed to work with teachers or students only receiving general education services because she was told her salary is paid with special education funds. As such, she politely explains to one of her middle school principals that she legally cannot respond to the crisis call to help a student who was found trying to commit suicide because the student is not one of hers (a student receiving special education services).

Step 1: List all applicable ethics codes and standards.	
Step 2: Describe why those codes and standards apply to the current situation and whether a violation has occurred based on those codes and standards.	
Step 3: Identify contributing factors, including one's own belief system, and actions that could have been taken to avoid the scenario.	
Step 4: Select the ethical course of action moving forward, as well as risk factors and continued monitoring needs.	

5 Scenarios for Confidentiality and Equity

Introduction

In this chapter, we will discuss Guiding Principles I.2 and I.3 of NASP's *Principles for Professional Ethics* (2020). While these principles are observed across the ethics codes of many psychological organizations and accrediting bodies, we will discuss the implications of these principles specifically for school psychologists. Many of our examples will center on the school setting, as that is where most school psychologists work. Schools can also be difficult settings in which to maintain these principles, given the significant amount of collaboration and, at times, lack of control over professional spaces and school-wide policy and procedure. As you read the chapter and work through the scenarios, we encourage you to consider how schools, or other settings, may introduce contributing variables to ethical dilemmas, and how you might work to eliminate these barriers in your own training and practice. In fact, as you go through all of the scenarios in this book, we encourage you to consider how you might have approached these situations from the onset to prevent ethical standards from being violated in the first place. Through our work as school psychology trainers, we encourage students to consider the pros and cons of a decision before being faced with the decision itself. This helps reduce the likelihood that decisions will be made based on social conformity rather than what is best for the student and in keeping with our ethical standards.

Guiding Principle I.2 Privacy and Confidentiality

Like all psychologists, school psychologists deal with sensitive information and have a responsibility to clients to handle that information with care. School psychologists seek out only information that is relevant to the services they provide to each client, and they respect clients' right to choose which information they want to disclose. School psychologists maintain privacy and confidentiality, disclosing information only when required by law and on a need-to-know basis or when given consent to disclose that information. As you will see in several of the scenarios in this chapter, schools can be difficult places to maintain confidentiality. Determining who needs to know information may be a daunting process at times, especially when others may believe they should have access to the information you gathered about the student and their family to provide services. School psychologists may need to explain to others the confidential boundaries of the data they collect, emphasizing that students and their families have federally granted rights to privacy of their educational records, which includes access to that information within schools (U.S. Department of Education, 2021). This is one such instance where law and ethics agree. Additionally, many school psychologists do not have consistent, or adequate,

DOI: 10.4324/9781003273950-5

office space, resulting in shared, or even public, spaces being the primary office space. This can pose problems for maintaining confidentiality during testing or other service provision, as well as for confidential record keeping. In these instances, school psychologists are encouraged to advocate for their needs and to explain the ethical, and legal, requirements of privacy and confidentiality.

School psychologists inform students and clients of the boundaries of confidentiality prior to providing services, and often throughout service provision. The latter portion of that sentence is particularly important, as clients or learners may forget what you can and cannot keep private over the course of the therapeutic or other relationship. Consent is an ongoing process, which includes reviewing both the services to be provided, as well as the boundaries of those services. Ethically, school psychologists also maintain privacy of health information, sexual orientation, and gender identity and expression of students, parents, and/or school employees. This is an instance where law and ethics may not always agree. For example, some states may have laws requiring education professionals to report information about a minor's sexual orientation or gender identity and expression to guardians, regardless of whether the minor wants the parent or guardian to know that information. School psychologists are encouraged to use a problem-solving process to determine legal and ethical standards when choosing when and what to disclose. Further, when law and ethics are in opposition, this may provide an opportunity for professional advocacy at the local and/or state level to promote law and policy that is supported by the research literature base and ethical guides within the field.

Guiding Principle I.3 Fairness, Equity, and Justice

School psychologists *actively* work to promote fairness and social justice. *The Principles for Professional Ethics* (2020), and the field of school psychology in general, has moved toward requiring active participation in activities to promote fairness and social justice. Whereas previously, it may have been acceptable to maintain status quo, expectations today are that school psychologists work to make schools fair and just communities where all students and families have equitable access to educational services. Additionally, school psychologists do not discriminate, or condone discrimination, against any person based on actual or perceived characteristics. When discrimination has occurred, school psychologists work to correct practices that led to discrimination, at the individual and systems levels. This includes restoring justice in situations where a wrong has occurred to an individual or group, as well as program evaluation to identify systems-level policies and practices that may be discriminatory so that they may be removed or altered.

As seen in current and historical events and recent research, systems historically have been set up in ways that do not encourage fairness or equity, and a number of systems continue to prevent fairness and equity through standards and expectations, access to diverse education, and more (for further, but not exhaustive, reading in this area: Blake et al., 2016; Rausch & Skiba, 2017; Sullivan et al., 2016). School psychologists must weigh professional ethics and responsibilities to students and families served, as well as legislation and policy, in order to promote fair and just actions in their school systems. This will require school psychologists to collaborate with other professionals and families, to engage in advocacy work, and to, at times, risk their own comfortability in the best interests of the school communities they serve. Of all the standards discussed so far, Guiding Principle I.3 (NASP, 2020) provides ample opportunities for advocacy for school psychology trainees and practitioners. If interested, your state school psychology organization is a great place to get started learning about and participating in advocacy work.

Let's Practice

Below are a set of case studies to help you familiarize yourself with potential ethical dilemmas in the areas of privacy and confidentiality and fairness, equity, and justice as a school psychologist. As always, we recommend completing the scenario worksheets collaboratively. When working collaboratively, there is opportunity for sharing different perspectives, which may ultimately lead to better problem-solving.

Reference List

Blake, J. J., Gregory, A., James, M., & Hasan, G. W. (2016). Early warning signs: Identifying opportunities to disrupt racial inequities in school discipline through data-based decision making. *School Psychology Forum: Research in Practice, 10*(3), 289–306.

National Association of School Psychologists. (2020). *The professional standards of the National Association of School Psychologists.* Retrieved May 1, 2021, from www.nasponline.org/x55315.xml

Rausch, M. K., & Skiba, R. J. (2017). Addressing disproportionately high rates of disciplinary removal for students of color: The need for systemic interventions. In E. C. Lopez, S. G. Nahari, & S. L. Proctor (Eds.), *Handbook of multicultural school psychology: An interdisciplinary perspective* (pp. 276–290). Routledge.

Sullivan, A. L., Artiles, A. J., & Hernandez-Saca, D. (2016). Systemic approaches to addressing disproportionality of culturally and linguistically diverse students in special education. In E. C. Lopez, S. G. Nahari, & S. L. Proctor (Eds.), *Handbook of multicultural school psychology: An interdisciplinary perspective* (pp. 306–322). Routledge.

U.S. Department of Education. (2021). *Family Educational Rights and Privacy Act (FERPA).* Retrieved January 20, 2022, from https://www2.ed.gov/policy/gen/guid/fpco/ferpa/index.html

Practice Scenarios

Scenario 1

During the course of a counseling session for test anxiety, Marcus Smith-Schuster reveals to the school psychologist that his father is transgender and has been living as a man for the past 20 years. The school psychologist, Mr. Dennison, finds this information interesting and puts it in his reports that he then places in Marcus' permanent file. The following year, after a request for educational records to help Marcus receive accommodations on the Scholastic Aptitude Test and American College Testing exams, Mr. Schuster is shocked to discover information about his gender identity in the reports. He is furious and is now threatening to sue the school district.

Step 1: List all applicable ethics codes and standards.	
Step 2: Describe why those codes and standards apply to the current situation and whether a violation has occurred based on those codes and standards.	
Step 3: Identify contributing factors, including one's own belief system, and actions that could have been taken to avoid the scenario.	
Step 4: Select the ethical course of action moving forward, as well as risk factors and continued monitoring needs.	

Scenario 2

You have been counseling a student who identifies themselves to you as transgender female this year. The student has not publicly identified as female to peers, other school staff, or family members and has asked that you keep their gender identity between the two of you until they are ready to share the information with others. During a meeting with the school team, you mistakenly use the student's preferred name and pronouns. When you realize your error, you ask those in the meeting to keep this to themselves and not tell others about the student's gender identity until they are ready to share.

Step 1: List all applicable ethics codes and standards.	
Step 2: Describe why those codes and standards apply to the current situation and whether a violation has occurred based on those codes and standards.	
Step 3: Identify contributing factors, including one's own belief system, and actions that could have been taken to avoid the scenario.	
Step 4: Select the ethical course of action moving forward, as well as risk factors and continued monitoring needs.	

Scenario 3

Mrs. McKendree, a school psychologist, has a long history of being a student advocate and recently helped a student denied special education eligibility for having HIV receive Section 504 services instead. However, when she discovers the boy with HIV is on the opposing track and field team as her son, she becomes frightened for the health of her son. Mrs. McKendree confronts the opposing coach and the referees about allowing someone living with HIV to participate in sports and demands the student be removed from the team roster.

Step 1: List all applicable ethics codes and standards.	
Step 2: Describe why those codes and standards apply to the current situation and whether a violation has occurred based on those codes and standards.	
Step 3: Identify contributing factors, including one's own belief system, and actions that could have been taken to avoid the scenario.	
Step 4: Select the ethical course of action moving forward, as well as risk factors and continued monitoring needs.	

Scenario 4

After long mornings filled with administering assessments and returning phone calls, Katie Cross likes to visit the teacher's lounge to eat her lunch and destress for a few moments. While eating her sandwich and discussing the anticipated firing of the wrestling coach with another teacher, Mr. Baker, the tenth-grade science teacher, walks in to purchase a soda from the vending machine. While waiting for the machine to drop his drink of choice, Mr. Baker asks Mrs. Cross how one of his students, Hunter, did on the cognitive assessment she pulled him from class to take earlier that morning. Mrs. Cross lets him know she is not done with the full evaluation yet but expects Hunter will qualify for services because of his poor performance on the cognitive assessment.

Step 1: List all applicable ethics codes and standards.	
Step 2: Describe why those codes and standards apply to the current situation and whether a violation has occurred based on those codes and standards.	
Step 3: Identify contributing factors, including one's own belief system, and actions that could have been taken to avoid the scenario.	
Step 4: Select the ethical course of action moving forward, as well as risk factors and continued monitoring needs.	

Scenario 5

You meet weekly with a 13-year-old student as part of their IEP to work on coping skills. At the beginning of the therapeutic relationship, you mentioned there could be a time you might have to tell the student's parents what is said in your meetings; however, you do not mention what types of information would need to be reported. During one of your meetings, the student shares that they have been self-medicating with painkillers several times a week for the past several months. When the student goes back to class, you immediately call their parents to share this information and discuss possible responses to stop the self-medication and keep the student safe. When the student learns that you told their parents about the medication use, they accuse you of lying and say they would not have shared the information if they had known you would tell their parents.

Step 1: List all applicable ethics codes and standards.	
Step 2: Describe why those codes and standards apply to the current situation and whether a violation has occurred based on those codes and standards.	
Step 3: Identify contributing factors, including one's own belief system, and actions that could have been taken to avoid the scenario.	
Step 4: Select the ethical course of action moving forward, as well as risk factors and continued monitoring needs.	

Scenario 6

While making copies in the workroom, which connects to the break room, you hear a teacher in the break room mimicking a student's speech articulation to a colleague. The teacher is complaining about the student's speech, stating that the parents should have sought speech services when the student was a toddler so that the teacher would not have to try to interpret what the student was saying now that they are in school. You are shocked, unsure what you should say to the teacher, and do not want to get on their bad side, so you finish making your copies and leave without saying anything.

Step 1: List all applicable ethics codes and standards.	
Step 2: Describe why those codes and standards apply to the current situation and whether a violation has occurred based on those codes and standards.	
Step 3: Identify contributing factors, including one's own belief system, and actions that could have been taken to avoid the scenario.	
Step 4: Select the ethical course of action moving forward, as well as risk factors and continued monitoring needs.	

Scenario 7

Dr. Linda Hall has been supervising school psychology practicum students whose course assignment was to complete a program evaluation. The students chose to examine disproportionality data for the district and found that Black female students were disproportionately identified as meeting criteria for emotional disturbance. They also found that manifestation determinations were more likely to find Black females' behavior as not being a manifestation of their disability when compared to White and Asian peers who committed similar offenses. Dr. Hall was distraught by these findings and has asked the superintendent if she can provide professional development about manifestation determinations and present the data compiled by the practicum students at the beginning of the year. She is also seeking permission to identify individuals within the community who can serve as cultural brokers between the school and the community to increase relations between the two.

Step 1: List all applicable ethics codes and standards.	
Step 2: Describe why those codes and standards apply to the current situation and whether a violation has occurred based on those codes and standards.	
Step 3: Identify contributing factors, including one's own belief system, and actions that could have been taken to avoid the scenario.	
Step 4: Select the ethical course of action moving forward, as well as risk factors and continued monitoring needs.	

Scenario 8

Ms. Elizaveta is completing her final practicum course before heading to internship. The most recent case her supervisor gave her is challenging her, though. After another difficult day trying to convince the teacher to provide more positive feedback to the student she is at her wits' end. So, she decides to seek consultation on a popular school psychology Facebook group. Elizaveta is careful to only disclose the grade, first names of the student and the teacher, and the student's presenting problem. After writing everything she has tried to get the teacher to do and providing direct quotes about the teacher's responses refusing to participate in the intervention, Elizaveta is emotionally distraught and ends the post by expressing her frustration with this teacher and all teachers who do not have the best interest of the children in their hearts and that she wishes they would quit teaching because they are not suited for the profession. Two weeks later her instructor meets with her privately to inform her that the school no longer wants her working on that campus. It turns out that a school psychologist working in a neighboring district is a close friend of the teacher and reported the post to her friend who then notified the school superintendent.

Step 1: List all applicable ethics codes and standards.	
Step 2: Describe why those codes and standards apply to the current situation and whether a violation has occurred based on those codes and standards.	
Step 3: Identify contributing factors, including one's own belief system, and actions that could have been taken to avoid the scenario.	
Step 4: Select the ethical course of action moving forward, as well as risk factors and continued monitoring needs.	

Scenario 9

You are working as a school psychologist in a rural area that has a history of discriminatory practices. While many of the visibly discriminatory practices are no longer standard policy and procedure in your district, many policies and unwritten rules that further marginalize minority students remain. You grew up in the area and have many former teachers on staff at the schools. Because of this, you often feel like you cannot speak out, as you would be disrespecting your former teachers, so you keep your head down and focus on your assigned cases. Over time, you feel less and less able to speak up and advocate for the systems-level changes needed to provide a fair and safe educational environment for all students.

Step 1: List all applicable ethics codes and standards.	
Step 2: Describe why those codes and standards apply to the current situation and whether a violation has occurred based on those codes and standards.	
Step 3: Identify contributing factors, including one's own belief system, and actions that could have been taken to avoid the scenario.	
Step 4: Select the ethical course of action moving forward, as well as risk factors and continued monitoring needs.	

Scenario 10

Dr. Mike Spears is alarmed by the growing number of students whose names he cannot pronounce at his new school district. In particular, he is concerned that many of these students and their families are here illegally. This is especially upsetting to Dr. Spears because the economy is in a recession and unemployment is the highest it has ever been, yet he has heard several other school personnel make comments about these parents working multiple jobs. Outraged that U.S. jobs are going to illegal workers and livid that illegal students who cannot keep up in the classroom could consume even more taxpayer dollars by seeking federal funding via special education status, Dr. Spears decides to assume the gatekeeper role with evaluation and deny special education eligibility to any student with a foreign-sounding name.

Step 1: List all applicable ethics codes and standards.	
Step 2: Describe why those codes and standards apply to the current situation and whether a violation has occurred based on those codes and standards.	
Step 3: Identify contributing factors, including one's own belief system, and actions that could have been taken to avoid the scenario.	
Step 4: Select the ethical course of action moving forward, as well as risk factors and continued monitoring needs.	

Scenario 11

During the course of a psychoeducational evaluation of a third-grade student referred for concerns about reading ability, you interview the student's mother. During the interview, the mother mentions that she used recreational drugs prior to, but not during her pregnancy with the student. When writing the assessment report, which will be part of the student's educational record, you include this information about prior drug use of the mother. The mother is upset when she sees the report, stating that this information was not necessary to include in the report, as it reflects poorly on her ability to parent and has nothing to do with her child's reading ability.

Step 1: List all applicable ethics codes and standards.	
Step 2: Describe why those codes and standards apply to the current situation and whether a violation has occurred based on those codes and standards.	
Step 3: Identify contributing factors, including one's own belief system, and actions that could have been taken to avoid the scenario.	
Step 4: Select the ethical course of action moving forward, as well as risk factors and continued monitoring needs.	

Scenario 12

During the COVID-19 pandemic, you are frequently observing in classrooms, both in-person and virtually, as teachers are asking for more consultation than usual to support their hybrid classroom environments. One morning, you walk into a kindergarten classroom and do not see the student you are meant to observe. You ask the teacher where they are, and the teacher tells you the student will be absent that week, and you reply, "Oh yes, I forgot they are sick." Following your statement, the students in the classroom begin asking questions about the student, their health status, and if they have the COVID-19 virus. You do your best to evade their questions and leave to complete the next item on your schedule.

Step 1: List all applicable ethics codes and standards.	
Step 2: Describe why those codes and standards apply to the current situation and whether a violation has occurred based on those codes and standards.	
Step 3: Identify contributing factors, including one's own belief system, and actions that could have been taken to avoid the scenario.	
Step 4: Select the ethical course of action moving forward, as well as risk factors and continued monitoring needs.	

Scenario 13

Raul Collins is an empathic school psychologist. He has a deep respect for families whose parents work multiple jobs to make ends meet and is understanding when they are not able to attend school meetings because they would lose their job if they asked for the time off. In order to make the system work for his students, Raul will occasionally take the IEP signature forms to the parent's place of work during his lunch for the parent to sign. Today, Raul is especially understanding because this student also has AIDS, and the cost of treatment is expensive for the parents. After obtaining the all the necessary signatures Raul is in a rush to return back to campus because he just received a crisis call. Raul absently places the student's special education folder on top of his car so he can unlock the door. Shortly after leaving the place of business, he notices a strange sight, papers fluttering behind him. It finally dawns on Raul the horror of what happened, that the pages blowing around the street and into the ditch where children are playing are the student's special education paperwork, consent for services, IEP, and psychoeducational report. After pulling over, he is relieved to see that other cars have also stopped to help him gather all the paperwork.

Step 1: List all applicable ethics codes and standards.	
Step 2: Describe why those codes and standards apply to the current situation and whether a violation has occurred based on those codes and standards.	
Step 3: Identify contributing factors, including one's own belief system, and actions that could have been taken to avoid the scenario.	
Step 4: Select the ethical course of action moving forward, as well as risk factors and continued monitoring needs.	

Scenario 14

Jacqueline Murphy has been working with a fourth-grade girl, Jesse, on social-emotional-behavioral (SEB) skills for the last four months and dutifully taking progress monitoring data. She is excited to present her data to the IEP team to show the vast improvement that Jesse has been making. Although the parents do not attend the meeting, Jesse's social worker who is employed by the state does attend the meeting to make sure Jesse is receiving the services agreed to in her IEP and to update the school on Jesse's current functioning. After Jacqueline presents her progress monitoring data and sets new SEB target goals with collaboration from the team, the social worker compliments Jacqueline and comments that she could really use a Jacqueline at all of her schools.

Step 1: List all applicable ethics codes and standards.	
Step 2: Describe why those codes and standards apply to the current situation and whether a violation has occurred based on those codes and standards.	
Step 3: Identify contributing factors, including one's own belief system, and actions that could have been taken to avoid the scenario.	
Step 4: Select the ethical course of action moving forward, as well as risk factors and continued monitoring needs.	

Scenario 15

The parents of a child you recently assessed call to ask you to share the psychoeducational evaluation report you completed with the child's pediatrician, as they are considering medication options for treatment. The parents request you send the report immediately and provide you with the pediatrician's contact information. You send the report to the pediatrician that afternoon with only oral consent from the parents. When your supervisor finds out, they formally reprimand you for breaking confidentiality of the student given that written consent to share information was not obtained from the parents.

Step 1: List all applicable ethics codes and standards.	
Step 2: Describe why those codes and standards apply to the current situation and whether a violation has occurred based on those codes and standards.	
Step 3: Identify contributing factors, including one's own belief system, and actions that could have been taken to avoid the scenario.	
Step 4: Select the ethical course of action moving forward, as well as risk factors and continued monitoring needs.	

6 Scenarios for Competence and Accountability

Introduction

School psychologists receive extensive training in the field prior to credentialing; however, school psychology is a constantly changing field. As our field evolves due to our changing roles in schools, policy changes, and a growing body of research, we are tasked with maintaining competence. The *Principles for Professional Ethics* Guiding Principle II.1 (NASP, 2020) requires school psychologists to only practice in the areas in which they are qualified, to recognize when personal problems may interfere with their ability to provide competent services and adjust accordingly, and to maintain competence through ongoing continuing education. Through self-reflection and evaluation, we begin to "know what we do not know" so that we can improve ourselves for the benefit of the children, families, and schools we serve.

Guiding Principle II.1 Competence

All graduate training programs have areas of strength and weakness. It is also common for individuals graduating from the same program, and who were part of the same cohort, to demonstrate different strengths and weaknesses. In part, this is due to individual preferences and differing field-based experiences across field-based supervisors. Rather than shy away from acknowledging programmatic or individual weaknesses, school psychologists should seek supervision or consultation to further their professional development before engaging in the provision of services they are not competent to provide. At times, it may also be appropriate to refer to other professionals. When other qualified professionals are not available in the area, it is the school psychologist's duty to discuss these issues with the parent(s) or guardian and seek resources to support their provision of care (e.g., supervision, professional development, consultation) when the student's needs would otherwise go unmet.

Attending conventions at the state and national level are two examples of common ways to gain professional development. However, we also encourage newly credentialed school psychologists to engage in a formal mentorship during their first year, at least. If this is not available at your district, one of the many NASP member perks is the NASP Mentorship Program (NASP, 2022), which provides a databank of other school psychologists who have indicated their willingness to mentor others as part of their service to the profession. NASP's recommendation is to engage in mentorship for at least one month, but they also encourage a year-long mentorship.

At times personal issues (e.g., illness, relationship problems, mental health issues, physical injuries) may encroach on one's ability to carry out their professional duties. Some of these issues, such as relationship problems, may create biases toward groups of

DOI: 10.4324/9781003273950-6

people that did not previously exist. This is another reason why having a strong collaborative network in place is important. These individuals may realize we are not performing at capacity and address these issues with us in a caring, but direct way. Regardless, it is the individual's responsibility to identify when personal problems impede one's delivery of services.

Guiding Principle II.2 Accepting Responsibility for Actions

Accountability is an increasingly important component of professional practice, and school psychologists are required to make decisions, revise those decisions as needed, and document decisions so that they may take responsibility for their actions. This includes ensuring documentation is accurate, monitoring progress of all recommendations and intervention plans for effectiveness, making appropriate recommendations, and correcting misunderstandings or ineffective recommendations. School psychologists actively attempt to mitigate harmful effects of their recommendations or services. When supervising graduate students' field experiences, such as practicum or internship, school psychologists accept responsibility for their supervisees' work. The Principle for Professional Ethics Guiding Principle II.2 Accepting Responsibility for Actions (NASP, 2020) ensures that school psychologists are thoughtful in their recommendations and follow-up to monitor for effectiveness. Overall, school psychologists accept responsibility for their actions and the actions of those they supervise.

There are several potential areas for ethical violations within this area. For example, over the course of one's career there may be times when a school psychologist is pressured to falsify records by backdating documents or asking relevant stakeholders to sign a backdated a document, particularly when a district expects to be audited by the state. Standard II.2.1 Accuracy of Documents (NASP, 2020) makes it clear that falsifying a document is unethical. To ethically remedy such instances, school psychologists should instead provide an addendum to the document. Further, in many instances, school psychologists may engage in a traditional assessment role and have little oversight of recommendation implementation. It is the school psychologist's responsibility to either personally gather progress monitoring data or delegate the collection of progress monitoring data for interventions or other recommendations they provide. Then, school psychologists must make decisions about continuing, modifying, or discontinuing the intervention based on the progress monitoring data collected.

When supervising graduate students, it is the supervisor's duty to ensure the supervisee is providing competent services. This is a large responsibility, as the supervisor's credential to practice could be jeopardized based on the actions of the supervisee. However, the supervisee should not be mistaken into believing any missteps would only affect the livelihood of their supervisor. Depending on the situation, the supervisee may also become ineligible to practice. To help prevent such situations, strong collaborative relationships between the supervisor and supervisee are recommended. Without individuals willing to give back to the field and supervise others, the critical workforce shortage will continue to worsen (NASP, 2021).

When miscommunications or errors occur, school psychologists should take responsibility for their actions and take remedial steps to rectify the negative outcomes of their actions or inactions. Throughout one's career it is unlikely that anyone will perform or act flawlessly. It is our reactions to our mistakes, taking responsibility for them, learning from them, and taking proactive steps to prevent them from occurring in the future that make us more trustworthy and valuable members to our respective communities.

Let's Practice

Below are a set of case studies to help you familiarize yourself with potential ethical dilemmas in the areas of competence and accepting responsibility for your actions as a school psychologist. As always, we recommend completing the scenario worksheets individually and then collaboratively. When working collaboratively, there is opportunity for sharing different perspectives, which may ultimately lead to better problem-solving.

Reference List

National Association of School Psychologists. (2020). *The professional standards of the National Association of School Psychologists.* Retrieved May 1, 2021, from www.nasponline.org/x55315.xml

National Association of School Psychologists. (2021). *Shortages in school psychology: Challenges to meeting the growing needs of U.S. students and schools* [Research summary]. Retrieved February 9, 2022, from www.nasponline.org/Documents/Research%20and%20Policy/Research%20Center/School_Psychology_Shortage.pdf

National Association of School Psychologists. (2022). *NASP mentorship program.* Retrieved February 9, 2022, from www.nasponline.org/mentorship

Practice Scenarios

Scenario 1

Jake Allyn, NCSP works in a state with legalized marijuana laws. Jake regularly takes advantage of this law on the weekends and after school hours. After the death of his dog, Jake's use of marijuana increased significantly, and it has become common knowledge at the school and in the community because he constantly smells of marijuana. Recently, parents have been requesting the special education director assign a different school psychologist to work with their child because they are concerned Jake is not fully functional in the workplace.

Step 1: List all applicable ethics codes and standards.	
Step 2: Describe why those codes and standards apply to the current situation and whether a violation has occurred based on those codes and standards.	
Step 3: Identify contributing factors, including one's own belief system, and actions that could have been taken to avoid the scenario.	
Step 4: Select the ethical course of action moving forward, as well as risk factors and continued monitoring needs.	

Scenario 2

Julie Hogshead is a school psychologist who loves to attend the NASP Convention each year to gain some continuing professional development (CPD) and to meet up with friends and colleagues. This year's Convention is in a location Julie has always wanted to visit, so she makes plans for several sightseeing activities during the trip. After the trip, Julie realizes she did not attend as many CPD sessions at the Convention as she needed to renew her NCSP credential with NASP. She decides to complete activity forms for some of the poster sessions offered at the Convention and claims CPD for them, even though she did not attend them.

Step 1: List all applicable ethics codes and standards.	
Step 2: Describe why those codes and standards apply to the current situation and whether a violation has occurred based on those codes and standards.	
Step 3: Identify contributing factors, including one's own belief system, and actions that could have been taken to avoid the scenario.	
Step 4: Select the ethical course of action moving forward, as well as risk factors and continued monitoring needs.	

Scenario 3

Berat Schwartz is a school psychologist who receives several independent evaluation reports completed by private practice school psychologists each year. There is one school psychologist, in particular, whose reports they dread, because the reports are often full of errors, such as using the wrong name, incorrect pronouns, and spelling and grammar errors. For example, on the most recent report Berat received, the school psychologist clearly used an old report as a template and left some of the previous names of the client and the client's teachers in the report instead of the current client's information.

Step 1: List all applicable ethics codes and standards.	
Step 2: Describe why those codes and standards apply to the current situation and whether a violation has occurred based on those codes and standards.	
Step 3: Identify contributing factors, including one's own belief system, and actions that could have been taken to avoid the scenario.	
Step 4: Select the ethical course of action moving forward, as well as risk factors and continued monitoring needs.	

Scenario 4

Courtnie Bull is a school psychologist in a large, urban district. Her training and previous experiences have helped Courtnie develop competence in several areas of service provision, but she struggles with counseling and therapy provision. Given that she does not feel she is competent, Courtnie seeks mentorship and supervision from the school district's lead school psychologist. The lead school psychologist of Courtnie's district tells her that they do not have time to supervise her, and that she should be prepared to provide any required services. Although Courtnie feels uncomfortable with it, she provides counseling and therapy services to her assigned students.

Step 1: List all applicable ethics codes and standards.	
Step 2: Describe why those codes and standards apply to the current situation and whether a violation has occurred based on those codes and standards.	
Step 3: Identify contributing factors, including one's own belief system, and actions that could have been taken to avoid the scenario.	
Step 4: Select the ethical course of action moving forward, as well as risk factors and continued monitoring needs.	

Scenario 5

Dr. Eun-Woo Yun is a school psychologist. As part of each psychoeducational assessment, Dr. Yun provides a list of recommendations, then works with school teams to put those recommendations in place. When others report to Dr. Yun that the recommendations are not working, she blames the implementers, saying they must not be doing something right because it is an evidence-based intervention. Dr. Yun tells them that she has completed her part, and now it is their time to see the recommendations through and implement them correctly.

Step 1: List all applicable ethics codes and standards.	
Step 2: Describe why those codes and standards apply to the current situation and whether a violation has occurred based on those codes and standards.	
Step 3: Identify contributing factors, including one's own belief system, and actions that could have been taken to avoid the scenario.	
Step 4: Select the ethical course of action moving forward, as well as risk factors and continued monitoring needs.	

Scenario 6

Dr. Shawn Enoch is a field-based supervisor for an APA-accredited internship program. This year, Dr. Enoch has an exceptionally talented and conscientious intern that Dr. Enoch has been supervising for the last eight months. Dr. Enoch is certain the intern, Jasmine, is an ethical and legal practitioner so he has no qualms telling the intern to sign reports by herself. He explains to Jasmine that part of the internship experience is to gain graduated experiences and to function with greater independence throughout the year. Although he has never recommended an intern solely sign reports, he believes that because of Jasmine's extraordinary exceptionalism that she is ready for this next step toward independence.

Step 1: List all applicable ethics codes and standards.	
Step 2: Describe why those codes and standards apply to the current situation and whether a violation has occurred based on those codes and standards.	
Step 3: Identify contributing factors, including one's own belief system, and actions that could have been taken to avoid the scenario.	
Step 4: Select the ethical course of action moving forward, as well as risk factors and continued monitoring needs.	

Scenario 7

Ten years ago, Ms. Ariella Eifert divorced Mr. Lucas Eifert. After the divorce, Mr. Eifert remarried and had a child, Bob, with Ms. Eifert's stepsister. Bob attends the same school Ms. Eifert works at as a school psychologist. Bob's teacher recently referred Bob for a functional behavioral assessment because he has been blurting out answers in class. After receiving consent to observe and consult with the teacher, Ms. Eifert recommended a full individual evaluation for emotional disturbance. At the IEP meeting, Ms. Eifert gleefully reviews the results of her evaluation where she highlights that Bob frequently blurts out answers without raising his hand, frequently requests to leave the class to use the restroom, and incessantly bounces his legs when sitting at his desk. Ms. Eifert uses this data to recommend Bob receive services under emotional disturbance and that he be moved to the behavioral unit.

Step 1: List all applicable ethics codes and standards.	
Step 2: Describe why those codes and standards apply to the current situation and whether a violation has occurred based on those codes and standards.	
Step 3: Identify contributing factors, including one's own belief system, and actions that could have been taken to avoid the scenario.	
Step 4: Select the ethical course of action moving forward, as well as risk factors and continued monitoring needs.	

Scenario 8

Mr. and Mrs. Webster, both school psychologists, opened a private tutoring service 15 years ago. The business has grown to include 20 additional employees. Last week, Mr. Webster found out Mrs. Webster has been having multiple affairs during at least the last five years. Distraught and angry, Mr. Webster has been sending company emails to all of the employees updating them with details about what happened and asking the employees to report any violations of company policies to him that they have observed Mrs. Webster to engage in, especially sexual harassment. None of the employees have reported any instances of policy violations, but a few have left the practice and cited the emails as the reason during the exit interview.

Step 1: List all applicable ethics codes and standards.	
Step 2: Describe why those codes and standards apply to the current situation and whether a violation has occurred based on those codes and standards.	
Step 3: Identify contributing factors, including one's own belief system, and actions that could have been taken to avoid the scenario.	
Step 4: Select the ethical course of action moving forward, as well as risk factors and continued monitoring needs.	

Scenario 9

Ms. Sherry Smeagol serves on the response to intervention (RTI) team for her campus. In this role and in her role as the school psychologist, she is responsible for recommending and implementing Tier III interventions. She meticulously designs each intervention based on the specific needs of the student and based on stakeholder feedback. Furthermore, she makes sure the interventions are culturally relevant. After the relevant stakeholders agree to the intervention, she trains the interventionists how to implement the intervention. At the end of each nine-week period, Ms. Smeagol and the team invite the teacher to the RTI Team meeting to report on how the student is doing.

Step 1: List all applicable ethics codes and standards.	
Step 2: Describe why those codes and standards apply to the current situation and whether a violation has occurred based on those codes and standards.	
Step 3: Identify contributing factors, including one's own belief system, and actions that could have been taken to avoid the scenario.	
Step 4: Select the ethical course of action moving forward, as well as risk factors and continued monitoring needs.	

Scenario 10

Mariah Blanchard is a school psychologist in a small school district. She is the only school psychologist for the district, so she completes several assessments each year, often more than 100. Since Mariah has such a high caseload, she often skips revising her reports and hopes for the best. Although she tries to make sure they are accurate, it is not uncommon for errors to make it into the final report.

Step 1: List all applicable ethics codes and standards.	
Step 2: Describe why those codes and standards apply to the current situation and whether a violation has occurred based on those codes and standards.	
Step 3: Identify contributing factors, including one's own belief system, and actions that could have been taken to avoid the scenario.	
Step 4: Select the ethical course of action moving forward, as well as risk factors and continued monitoring needs.	

Scenario 11

Mr. Byron Fernandez has collected a bank of recommendations over the years and has sorted them into recommendations by disability category. Whenever Mr. Fernandez completes a psychoeducational evaluation, he inserts the recommendations for the specific disability category indicated for the student, regardless of the appropriateness of the recommendations for that particular student. Because of this, Mr. Fernandez's recommendations can, at times, be inappropriate, contraindicated by the data, and outdated or not evidence-based. When asked by a colleague why he does not prepare individual recommendations, Mr. Fernandez states that nobody follows his recommendations anyway.

Step 1: List all applicable ethics codes and standards.	
Step 2: Describe why those codes and standards apply to the current situation and whether a violation has occurred based on those codes and standards.	
Step 3: Identify contributing factors, including one's own belief system, and actions that could have been taken to avoid the scenario.	
Step 4: Select the ethical course of action moving forward, as well as risk factors and continued monitoring needs.	

Scenario 12

Mr. Drew Forsyth has been a school psychologist for the past 12 years and has become bored doing evaluations with children. His state recently changed their laws to allow those with his training and credentials to work in private practice. Excited about this change, Mr. Forsyth immediately signs on with a local mental health clinic and begins offering to provide counseling services to adults diagnosed with Anorexia Nervosa and to those who have experienced complex trauma.

Step 1: List all applicable ethics codes and standards.	
Step 2: Describe why those codes and standards apply to the current situation and whether a violation has occurred based on those codes and standards.	
Step 3: Identify contributing factors, including one's own belief system, and actions that could have been taken to avoid the scenario.	
Step 4: Select the ethical course of action moving forward, as well as risk factors and continued monitoring needs.	

Scenario 13

Macsen Parks, NCSP has decided to take on his first practicum student this year and is really excited to have an extra pair of hands to help out. Since Mr. Parks' practicum student has liability insurance, he assumes that the student maintains some responsibility over their own work. Mr. Parks also knows the training program this student attends is well-known for their students' report-writing abilities. To help himself out, Mr. Parks asks the practicum student to write several reports for him using assessment data Mr. Parks has already collected. Given that the student's school psychology graduate program is so well-known for report writing, Mr. Parks only skims over the practicum students' reports to make sure they are acceptable. Unfortunately, the practicum student has made several major errors in multiple reports that Mr. Parks did not catch and correct. When presented with these errors by a colleague, Mr. Parks blames the practicum student, stating that they actually wrote the reports.

Step 1: List all applicable ethics codes and standards.	
Step 2: Describe why those codes and standards apply to the current situation and whether a violation has occurred based on those codes and standards.	
Step 3: Identify contributing factors, including one's own belief system, and actions that could have been taken to avoid the scenario.	
Step 4: Select the ethical course of action moving forward, as well as risk factors and continued monitoring needs.	

Scenario 14

Ms. Veronica Weathers is a school psychologist serving a district with a school psychology to student ratio of 6,348:1. Suffice it to say, Ms. Weathers is extremely overworked and struggles to meet deadlines. At the last meeting she went to for a student, Dikembe, she realized during the meeting that she failed to provide reading recommendations. In order to save face, she explained that she did not provide recommendations because the initial referral was for inattentiveness and the student really should have gone through the dyslexia specialist instead of her for a reading evaluation. Although disappointed, the parents and the rest of team seemed to accept this news and moved forward with completing the paperwork for an evaluation for dyslexia.

Step 1: List all applicable ethics codes and standards.	
Step 2: Describe why those codes and standards apply to the current situation and whether a violation has occurred based on those codes and standards.	
Step 3: Identify contributing factors, including one's own belief system, and actions that could have been taken to avoid the scenario.	
Step 4: Select the ethical course of action moving forward, as well as risk factors and continued monitoring needs.	

Scenario 15

Ms. Kamps, NCSP is a new school psychologist and is living paycheck to paycheck to pay off her student loans as quickly as possible. In order to save money and time, she attends the NASP Convention every year to accrue CPD hours to maintain her NCSP credential. In order to make the most of her resources she quickly browses through each poster session in about ten minutes and then documents 1.5 hours for each session because that is the length of each poster session listed in the convention program. Ms. Kamps then attends a paper presentation, during each poster session, and documents that additional hour as well.

Step 1: List all applicable ethics codes and standards.	
Step 2: Describe why those codes and standards apply to the current situation and whether a violation has occurred based on those codes and standards.	
Step 3: Identify contributing factors, including one's own belief system, and actions that could have been taken to avoid the scenario.	
Step 4: Select the ethical course of action moving forward, as well as risk factors and continued monitoring needs.	

7 Scenarios for Direct Service Provision

Introduction

In this chapter, we will discuss and provide practice scenarios for Guiding Principle II.3 of NASP's *Principles for Professional Ethics* (2020), which falls under Broad Theme II, Professional Competence and Responsibility. Assessment and intervention practices are the primary direct services school psychologists provide and are encompassed by several of the NASP Practice Model Domains (NASP, 2020). Due to the overlap between the Practice Domains and the *Principles for Professional Ethics,* we encourage you to consider both best practices (e.g., research- and evidence-based practice) in the field, as well as the ethical standards discussed next when engaging in assessment and intervention practices.

Guiding Principle II.3 Responsible Assessment and Intervention Practices

As assessment and intervention are large parts of the roles of school psychologists, it should not be surprising that there are 14 standards in Guiding Principle II.3 (NASP, 2020). The assessment ethical standards include considerations school psychologists need to make prior to disability or special education eligibility determination, considerations around selecting instruments and the techniques and norms/standards used to administer them and interpret results, as well as guidance on using existing records to make decisions. Intervention ethical standards include the selection of evidence-based practices using a problem-solving framework. A notable inclusion are standards on the social validity of intervention selection, including both parental involvement and student assent and involvement.

Additionally, the standards in this section include some equity and fairness considerations, particularly around instrument validity and use of interpreters, as well as the previously mentioned parent involvement and student assent. These ethical standards require school psychologists to step away from use of a standard test battery for similar referral concerns and toward collecting and using ecological validity data to select appropriate assessment instruments, recommendations, and interventions. Part of being an ethical school psychologist is ensuring the assessments and instruments that are selected for use are appropriate for each individual student. In particular, it is important to only engage in research-based practices that are implemented in a manner consistent with their intended purpose. Further, it is the authors' experiences that many training programs do not teach the full spectrum of possible assessment instruments. This may be partially due to instructor or regional preference, but it would also be a daunting task to teach all possible technically sound assessment instruments within a small series of

DOI: 10.4324/9781003273950-7

courses. Therefore, selecting appropriate instruments requires school psychologists to engage in ongoing professional development and continuing education in order to know the available instruments, along with their purposes and limitations, as well as the unique characteristics and needs of the individual to be assessed.

School psychologists are also personally responsible for ensuring that standardization procedures are followed, and the results are communicated in an understandable way. As a school psychology student, you likely took/have taken multiple assessment courses where you were taught about, and practiced, the standardized administration of a variety of tests. Many of the practice opportunities provided through this training are best case scenario experiences, where you might practice with a peer, friend or family member, or typically developing child. However, in practice, the students and clients you will assess may struggle with following the directions you give during an assessment and need additional supports for a variety of reasons. School psychologists must balance student ability and support needs while maintaining standardization.

New to this section in the 2020 *Principles for Professional Ethics* are standards that have technology related updates. Tablets, telehealth, and virtual reality were never mentioned in the 2010 *Principles for Professional Ethics* but are represented in the 2020 update as technology has continued to advance and change the way we assess, deliver results, and administer interventions. In addition to the onward march of technological advancements within our field, the COVID-19 pandemic has served as a catalyst for many practitioners to engage technology (e.g., teleconsultation, teleintervention) to deliver services in a way they may never have before. Despite unforeseen or unexpected changes and events, practitioners are still obligated to uphold these ethical standards.

Let's Practice

Below are a set of case studies to help you familiarize yourself with potential ethical dilemmas in the areas of responsible assessment and intervention practices. As always, we recommend completing the scenario worksheets individually and then collaboratively. When working collaboratively, there is opportunity for sharing different perspectives, which may ultimately lead to better problem-solving.

Reference List

National Association of School Psychologists. (2020). *The professional standards of the National Association of School Psychologists.* Retrieved May 1, 2021, from www.nasponline.org/x55315.xml

Practice Scenarios

Scenario 1

Mark Moriarty, NCSP routinely administers the same cognitive assessment twice to students he evaluates. The first time he administers the assessment is to test the student's limits and the second time is according to standardization procedures. Mark does the assessment in this order, one day apart, because he previously noted that students were fatigued and less motivated when he attempted to test the limits only after giving the assessment in a standardized fashion. Mark reckons that by first testing the limits, he will get a better estimate of the individual's true cognitive capacity, which will allow him to make more informed recommendations to parents and teachers.

Step 1: List all applicable ethics codes and standards.	
Step 2: Describe why those codes and standards apply to the current situation and whether a violation has occurred based on those codes and standards.	
Step 3: Identify contributing factors, including one's own belief system, and actions that could have been taken to avoid the scenario.	
Step 4: Select the ethical course of action moving forward, as well as risk factors and continued monitoring needs.	

Scenario 2

Dr. Sellen is a school psychologist at a private practice where they complete psychoeducational assessments. They are currently using the third editions of the Woodcock-Johnson Tests of Cognitive Abilities and Tests of Achievement, even though the fourth editions have been available for several years. They feel that the tests did not change that much and that the tests are still valid to be used in decision-making, along with their clinical judgment.

Step 1: List all applicable ethics codes and standards.	
Step 2: Describe why those codes and standards apply to the current situation and whether a violation has occurred based on those codes and standards.	
Step 3: Identify contributing factors, including one's own belief system, and actions that could have been taken to avoid the scenario.	
Step 4: Select the ethical course of action moving forward, as well as risk factors and continued monitoring needs.	

Scenario 3

Ms. Plunkett is a school psychologist at a small, rural school. Unfortunately, poor funding has led to budget cuts and the school was not able to purchase updated and replacement materials for assessments. Although Ms. Plunkett has told her supervisors she needs the most up-to-date versions of assessments, the school recommended she locate free resources to be used instead. Ms. Plunkett located several social-emotional-behavioral rating scales online and is using them in place of published measures. She is not sure about the reliability or validity of these measures given that there is no published data, but she feels she has no other option.

Step 1: List all applicable ethics codes and standards.	
Step 2: Describe why those codes and standards apply to the current situation and whether a violation has occurred based on those codes and standards.	
Step 3: Identify contributing factors, including one's own belief system, and actions that could have been taken to avoid the scenario.	
Step 4: Select the ethical course of action moving forward, as well as risk factors and continued monitoring needs.	

Scenario 4

As standard operating procedure, Dr. Jayden Harper excludes students from meetings when discussing behavior plans and/or academic interventions that will soon be implemented. He does this because he is afraid if the student knows what is happening and how to access reinforcement it will decrease their intrinsic motivation to engage in the desired behavior.

Step 1: List all applicable ethics codes and standards.	
Step 2: Describe why those codes and standards apply to the current situation and whether a violation has occurred based on those codes and standards.	
Step 3: Identify contributing factors, including one's own belief system, and actions that could have been taken to avoid the scenario.	
Step 4: Select the ethical course of action moving forward, as well as risk factors and continued monitoring needs.	

Scenario 5

The school psychologists at The Ebbinghaus School for the Blind are well versed on how to administer valid assessments for blind students. Recently, a refugee family from Afghanistan enrolled their son, Bibi, in the school. In order to convey Bibi's assessment results to the parents, Bibi's older brother, Abdul, served as a translator. The family was very complimentary and thanked the school's assessment team repeatedly.

Step 1: List all applicable ethics codes and standards.	
Step 2: Describe why those codes and standards apply to the current situation and whether a violation has occurred based on those codes and standards.	
Step 3: Identify contributing factors, including one's own belief system, and actions that could have been taken to avoid the scenario.	
Step 4: Select the ethical course of action moving forward, as well as risk factors and continued monitoring needs.	

Scenario 6

Ms. Kleffer is a school psychologist in a district that primarily serves Hispanic/Latinx students, although the educational staff is primarily White. Ms. Kleffer has recently completed an assessment for a third-grade English learner and recommended that the student did not qualify for services with a Specific Learning Disability, because the student's language proficiency could not be ruled out as a cause of his learning struggles. Instead, she recommended English language learner (ELL) services and tiered intervention. She received significant persuasion efforts from the rest of the team to change her findings so the student could receive special education services. Given that the student was struggling, and Ms. Kleffer thought the student would benefit from additional services and wanted to avoid clashing with the team, she edited her report to recommend special education services under the Specific Learning Disability category.

Step 1: List all applicable ethics codes and standards.	
Step 2: Describe why those codes and standards apply to the current situation and whether a violation has occurred based on those codes and standards.	
Step 3: Identify contributing factors, including one's own belief system, and actions that could have been taken to avoid the scenario.	
Step 4: Select the ethical course of action moving forward, as well as risk factors and continued monitoring needs.	

Scenario 7

Mr. Kim Nolen is a school psychologist in a large urban district. Over his career, he has noticed a decline in parental involvement and interest in their children's education. He has become embittered and often complains about parents, in general, to others. Because of his observations and beliefs, he no longer contacts parents or involves them in the assessment or intervention process, aside from gaining necessary consent. He feels that it would be a waste of his time because the parents are unlikely to be available or involved anyway.

Step 1: List all applicable ethics codes and standards.	
Step 2: Describe why those codes and standards apply to the current situation and whether a violation has occurred based on those codes and standards.	
Step 3: Identify contributing factors, including one's own belief system, and actions that could have been taken to avoid the scenario.	
Step 4: Select the ethical course of action moving forward, as well as risk factors and continued monitoring needs.	

Scenario 8

Filipe Santos is thrilled to be a school psychologist during the digital age. He scours the internet for any and all virtual reality programs he can incorporate into interventions and assessments. Most recently, he has begun using a virtual reality program for conversion therapy. He is more comfortable using this approach given that his training program did not teach him how to perform conversion therapy and he can simply give the student a headset to wear and then print out the results to place in the student's file.

Step 1: List all applicable ethics codes and standards.	
Step 2: Describe why those codes and standards apply to the current situation and whether a violation has occurred based on those codes and standards.	
Step 3: Identify contributing factors, including one's own belief system, and actions that could have been taken to avoid the scenario.	
Step 4: Select the ethical course of action moving forward, as well as risk factors and continued monitoring needs.	

Scenario 9

Marita Jones is a new school psychologist building her intervention toolkit. She has lost access to her university's library database and is unfamiliar with NASP's publication access. Instead of searching the peer-reviewed literature for evidence-based interventions, she has been using open-access social media sites for ideas and materials. Marita has found some very cute ideas for counseling services and has started using some of these practices with students. While the students do not seem to be making progress, they seem to enjoy spending the time with her, so Marita continues using these practices and even recommends them to others.

Step 1: List all applicable ethics codes and standards.	
Step 2: Describe why those codes and standards apply to the current situation and whether a violation has occurred based on those codes and standards.	
Step 3: Identify contributing factors, including one's own belief system, and actions that could have been taken to avoid the scenario.	
Step 4: Select the ethical course of action moving forward, as well as risk factors and continued monitoring needs.	

Scenario 10

Luna Joy loves her job as a private practitioner. The only part that is difficult is when she evaluates a student who speaks Spanish. Because the area she lives in is 95% White and monolingual, it is very difficult to find someone who can interpret the evaluation results to the parents. In order to provide these services, Luna has to pay her sister in-law, who took four years of Spanish in college, to interpret the results. This has placed a strain on her personal relationship with her sister and sister in-law because Luna cannot afford to compensate at the same hourly rate as the law firm where her sister in-law works.

Step 1: List all applicable ethics codes and standards.	
Step 2: Describe why those codes and standards apply to the current situation and whether a violation has occurred based on those codes and standards.	
Step 3: Identify contributing factors, including one's own belief system, and actions that could have been taken to avoid the scenario.	
Step 4: Select the ethical course of action moving forward, as well as risk factors and continued monitoring needs.	

Scenario 11

Dr. Kleats is a school psychologist with a private practice where he completes several psychoeducational evaluations each year. While his evaluations are incredibly comprehensive, his clients have difficulty understanding his reports. They are often 30+ pages long, and he uses only professional terminology, with very little interpretation in plain language. Additionally, his summaries and recommendations are long and not clear. Clients typically leave feedback meetings confused and unsure of what next steps to take regarding the results.

Step 1: List all applicable ethics codes and standards.	
Step 2: Describe why those codes and standards apply to the current situation and whether a violation has occurred based on those codes and standards.	
Step 3: Identify contributing factors, including one's own belief system, and actions that could have been taken to avoid the scenario.	
Step 4: Select the ethical course of action moving forward, as well as risk factors and continued monitoring needs.	

Scenario 12

Jessica Buckey is becoming concerned about her supervisee, Abebe. During their last supervision meeting, Jessica asked Abebe why he did not correct the parents' misconception that percentile scores are the same as percentage points. Abebe explained that he finds it easier to get parents to agree to his eligibility recommendations when they believe the score reflects the percentage of items correct on the assessment and that it really does not make a difference anyway because the parents at this school are unlikely to understand the difference.

Step 1: List all applicable ethics codes and standards.	
Step 2: Describe why those codes and standards apply to the current situation and whether a violation has occurred based on those codes and standards.	
Step 3: Identify contributing factors, including one's own belief system, and actions that could have been taken to avoid the scenario.	
Step 4: Select the ethical course of action moving forward, as well as risk factors and continued monitoring needs.	

Scenario 13

Mr. Suiss is a school psychologist in a large district with significant staffing shortages. Given these shortages, Mr. Suiss' assessment caseload is very high, and he struggles to maintain the required timelines. When he is especially behind schedule or when he believes a case is straightforward, he collects very little assessment data from one or two sources and makes decisions. While he knows best practice includes collecting data from a variety of sources, he feels like he is not able to follow best practices in his current situation.

Step 1: List all applicable ethics codes and standards.	
Step 2: Describe why those codes and standards apply to the current situation and whether a violation has occurred based on those codes and standards.	
Step 3: Identify contributing factors, including one's own belief system, and actions that could have been taken to avoid the scenario.	
Step 4: Select the ethical course of action moving forward, as well as risk factors and continued monitoring needs.	

Scenario 14

During the COVID-19 pandemic, Mr. Johnson's school did not allow in-person assessments. Instead, the school recommended all re-evaluations be completed using only data collected from record reviews. Mr. Johnson used only the most recent evaluation report to make his recommendations, and it is not clear from the recommendations why the evaluation was conducted via record review and what limitations these recommendations may have.

Step 1: List all applicable ethics codes and standards.	
Step 2: Describe why those codes and standards apply to the current situation and whether a violation has occurred based on those codes and standards.	
Step 3: Identify contributing factors, including one's own belief system, and actions that could have been taken to avoid the scenario.	
Step 4: Select the ethical course of action moving forward, as well as risk factors and continued monitoring needs.	

Scenario 15

Dr. Plester, a private practice school psychologist, completes several assessments each year. Given that she works in private practice, she often only communicates with the parents and children. Although she misses out on information from the school setting, Dr. Plester feels that the parents know their child best and are the only important source of data, although her recommendations include services to be provided in the school setting.

Step 1: List all applicable ethics codes and standards.	
Step 2: Describe why those codes and standards apply to the current situation and whether a violation has occurred based on those codes and standards.	
Step 3: Identify contributing factors, including one's own belief system, and actions that could have been taken to avoid the scenario.	
Step 4: Select the ethical course of action moving forward, as well as risk factors and continued monitoring needs.	

8 Scenarios for Records and Materials

Introduction

School psychologists, with school administrators, maintain records of student data as a way to document decisions and services. There are various guidelines at the organizational, state, and federal levels on where records should be kept, how long they should be maintained, and who should be allowed to access them. In fact, the authors of this book have seen several posts in listservs and professional social media groups inquiring about the length of time records should be maintained and if parents have a right to see testing materials under copyright protection, often with varying answers. While we will not clear up the absolute answer to all these questions here, we will summarize the guidance from NASP (2020) about responsible record keeping. Keep in mind, NASP Guiding Principle II.4 (NASP, 2020) is specific to school-based record keeping, so those who do not work in schools should consider guidance specific to their setting.

Guiding Principle II.4 Responsible School-Based Record Keeping

Guiding Principle II.4 (NASP, 2020) indicates parents and students should be notified of their rights regarding their records and given access to their records when requested. Records should be comprehensive, providing enough detail to be useful in decision-making to other professionals and to serve as justification in the case of legal proceedings. A general rule of thumb when considering whether enough detail is provided in the records is to engage in perspective taking and consider if you were to receive the same records on a transfer student to your district, would you know what services to provide based on the information contained therein or would you have to gather more data, possibly repeating the exact same data-gathering procedures the student recently went through and ultimately delaying access to needed services?

While records must be comprehensive, only information relevant to the provision of school services should be included. At times, parents or guardians may provide the school psychologists with additional personal information about the family that is not relevant to providing the student services, so school psychologists must be familiar with ecological variables contributing to student functioning in order to selectively include relevant information in records. Test protocols should be included, and to answer an earlier question, yes, parents have the right to view their child's responses on test protocols, even when this conflicts with publisher guidance (Standard II.4.4). School personnel may also be given access to student records if they have a need to access the files for service provision. When electronic files are kept, school psychologists safeguard their privacy by using passwords and encryption and ensure equipment failure does not result in loss of records. Use of passwords and encryptions may be a foreign concept to some graduate

DOI: 10.4324/9781003273950-8

students or even seasoned professionals. Nonetheless, even as practicum students and interns, these tools need to be used to maintain privacy of records. This is especially important if you are sending your field-based supervisor and/or university-based supervisor reports to be reviewed remotely. For those unfamiliar with different types of passwords and encryptions available and their respective pros and cons, see American Psychological Association (2020) for a brief primer. School psychologists are also tasked with making sure electronic files are not stored in only one location. This requirement prevents loss of information from occurring and a student's services from being disrupted or delayed if a jump drive is lost, destroyed, or simply stops working. For example, something as seemingly easy to do as leaving one's thumb drive in a pants or shirt pocket that goes through the wash could destroy all the stored data. If this is the only location you had saved your report and the eligibility meeting is the next morning, the student's services (or your night's rest) could be greatly disrupted. A more recent consideration is the increasing number of cyber criminals targeting school records with ransomware attacks (U.S. Government Accountability Office, 2021).

School psychologists may also keep sole possession records, which are typically notes used by the school psychologist as a memory aid and are not accessible to others; however, if the note was used in decision-making, it should be included in the record. Finally, NASP (2020) does not indicate how long school-based records should be kept. Rather, guidance requires school psychologists to work with their administrators and others to create and enforce district policies that ensure the privacy of records, access to those only with rights or permission to access records, and timelines for the review and destruction of obsolete records in accordance with state laws. Additionally, NASP (2020) recommends school psychologists advocate that only final drafts of documents are included in student records.

Guiding Principle II.5 Responsible Use of Materials

School psychologists frequently use materials that are covered under copyright protection, including tests, protocols, intervention materials, publications, and more. The creators and/or publishers of these materials have intellectual property rights that school psychologists should respect. Guiding Principle II.5 (NASP, 2020) states that school psychologists work to maintain test security by only allowing those with rights or permissions to access test protocols and other materials. Parents are allowed to view their child's responses, as covered earlier. While typically they are not allowed copies, in the event where copies are required by law or district policy, they can be provided. Qualified professionals (e.g., school psychologists, psychologists) may also be given copies of protocols when written permission is given by the parent or guardian. Additionally, school psychologists do not support the use of restricted tests by those who are not qualified to use them.

Let's Practice

Below are a set of case studies to help you familiarize yourself with potential ethical dilemmas in the areas of responsible school-based record keeping and use of materials. As always, we recommend completing the scenario worksheets individually and then collaboratively. When working collaboratively, there is opportunity for sharing different perspectives, which may ultimately lead to better problem-solving.

Reference List

American Psychological Association. (2020, December 1). *ABCs and 123s of encryption: Here's what practitioners need to consider about data encryption and why it's important.* Retrieved February 9, 2022, from www.apaservices.org/practice/business/technology/data-encryption

National Association of School Psychologists. (2020). *The professional standards of the National Association of School Psychologists.* Retrieved May 1, 2021, from www.nasponline.org/x55315.xml

U.S. Government Accountability Office. (2021, November 21). *Critical infrastructure protection: Education should take additional steps to help protect K-12 schools from cyber threats.* Retrieved February 24, 2022, from www.gao.gov/products/gao-22-105024

Practice Scenarios

Scenario 1

Mr. Kurtis Priory is a school psychologist in a small rural district. At his schools, student records are held in the main school offices in file cabinets, and the school secretaries oversee access to files, as per district policy developed by school administrators with Mr. Priory's advice. While the school secretaries are very good at only sharing records with those outside of the schools who have permission, they often allow any school personnel to access student records, without asking why they need to see them.

Step 1: List all applicable ethics codes and standards.	
Step 2: Describe why those codes and standards apply to the current situation and whether a violation has occurred based on those codes and standards.	
Step 3: Identify contributing factors, including one's own belief system, and actions that could have been taken to avoid the scenario.	
Step 4: Select the ethical course of action moving forward, as well as risk factors and continued monitoring needs.	

Scenario 2

Dr. Silas Robinson is the lead school psychologist at Ginsburg Independent School District (ISD). In order to manage the most recent budget shortfall he has made 15 copies of the Stanford-Binet 5 protocol for each school psychologist in the district and instructed them to use these when assessing a student for an intellectual disability for the rest of the year or until the 6th edition is released. He cannot justify spending additional funds on an assessment that has not been updated since 2003.

Step 1: List all applicable ethics codes and standards.	
Step 2: Describe why those codes and standards apply to the current situation and whether a violation has occurred based on those codes and standards.	
Step 3: Identify contributing factors, including one's own belief system, and actions that could have been taken to avoid the scenario.	
Step 4: Select the ethical course of action moving forward, as well as risk factors and continued monitoring needs.	

Scenario 3

Ms. Daria Swanson is a school psychologist whose district has recently purchased a digital record keeping subscription. The district's administrators and personnel are excited, as this will simplify their record keeping system and allow for quick access by those who need to view student records. However, parents have not been notified about the change to record keeping in the district. Daria plans to notify parents only when they reach out to inquire about access to their child's records.

Step 1: List all applicable ethics codes and standards.	
Step 2: Describe why those codes and standards apply to the current situation and whether a violation has occurred based on those codes and standards.	
Step 3: Identify contributing factors, including one's own belief system, and actions that could have been taken to avoid the scenario.	
Step 4: Select the ethical course of action moving forward, as well as risk factors and continued monitoring needs.	

Scenario 4

The teachers at one of Ms. Edith Oliver's schools are interested in learning more about the tests she administers to students. Ms. Oliver decides to hold an informal meeting after school one day, where she reviews the tests she uses most often, and allow the teachers to open test kits to look through the materials and hand out blank test protocols for them to view. During the meeting, some teachers take photos of the materials and begin using some of the activities and questions in their classrooms.

Step 1: List all applicable ethics codes and standards.	
Step 2: Describe why those codes and standards apply to the current situation and whether a violation has occurred based on those codes and standards.	
Step 3: Identify contributing factors, including one's own belief system, and actions that could have been taken to avoid the scenario.	
Step 4: Select the ethical course of action moving forward, as well as risk factors and continued monitoring needs.	

Scenario 5

Wilson Block, a school psychologist, has just had a meeting with parents of a student on his caseload. The student, who receives special education services under the category of Specific Learning Disability, has recently turned 18. The parents have informed Mr. Block that their child has suddenly taken an interest in his education, specifically related to his disability, and wants to see his school records. The parents have asked Mr. Block not to share the records with their son, despite his aging into adulthood. Mr. Block agrees that the student is not ready to see the records. When the student contacts Mr. Block about seeing the records, Mr. Block tells him only his parents are allowed to see the file.

Step 1: List all applicable ethics codes and standards.	
Step 2: Describe why those codes and standards apply to the current situation and whether a violation has occurred based on those codes and standards.	
Step 3: Identify contributing factors, including one's own belief system, and actions that could have been taken to avoid the scenario.	
Step 4: Select the ethical course of action moving forward, as well as risk factors and continued monitoring needs.	

Scenario 6

Dr. Shanay Loblolly is a retired school psychologist who now works as a parent advocate. Zie was recently appalled that Dursley ISD would not allow zieself or the student's parent to inspect the test protocols used during the evaluation. Dr. Loblolly is concerned the evaluation was not performed correctly and suspects the protocol may have been scored incorrectly but is unsure what recourse the parents can take without being able to inspect the documents. The stance of the school is that the materials are copyrighted and by showing anyone else the protocols the district would be causing irreparable harm to the integrity of the assessment instrument.

Step 1: List all applicable ethics codes and standards.	
Step 2: Describe why those codes and standards apply to the current situation and whether a violation has occurred based on those codes and standards.	
Step 3: Identify contributing factors, including one's own belief system, and actions that could have been taken to avoid the scenario.	
Step 4: Select the ethical course of action moving forward, as well as risk factors and continued monitoring needs.	

Scenario 7

At the university clinic, Dr. Marc Jones routinely supervises practicum and internship students. Because of the COVID-19 pandemic, Dr. Jones agreed to allow first-semester students to complete the shadow practicum associated with their Introduction to School Psychology course at the clinic. Although the students only assignment for the course is to complete observations and interviews with professionals, Dr. Jones has asked one of the most promising students to administer a projective test on an 18-year-old client referred for schizophrenia because three of his interns were in quarantine.

Step 1: List all applicable ethics codes and standards.	
Step 2: Describe why those codes and standards apply to the current situation and whether a violation has occurred based on those codes and standards.	
Step 3: Identify contributing factors, including one's own belief system, and actions that could have been taken to avoid the scenario.	
Step 4: Select the ethical course of action moving forward, as well as risk factors and continued monitoring needs.	

Scenario 8

Kelli Jiu is a practicum student completing her hours at Harding ISD and at a local clinic, Sequoia Psychological Services. Kelli is careful to password protect and encrypt reports sent to her supervisor at Sequoia Psychological Services. In order to protect confidentiality, she uses a different password for each client and includes it in the body of the email so her supervisor will be able to access it easily. Because Kelli was provided with an ISD email address, Kelli does not encrypt or password protect documents when emailing psychoeducational reports to her supervisor at Harding ISD.

Step 1: List all applicable ethics codes and standards.	
Step 2: Describe why those codes and standards apply to the current situation and whether a violation has occurred based on those codes and standards.	
Step 3: Identify contributing factors, including one's own belief system, and actions that could have been taken to avoid the scenario.	
Step 4: Select the ethical course of action moving forward, as well as risk factors and continued monitoring needs.	

Scenario 9

Dr. Lena Gordon is an early career school psychologist who is extremely nervous about her assessments being challenged in a due process. She has heard stories of some psychologists' records containing potentially biased information that led to their results being called into question. For this reason, she keeps her records as minimal as possible, sometimes leaving out information that was crucial in her decision-making process.

Step 1: List all applicable ethics codes and standards.	
Step 2: Describe why those codes and standards apply to the current situation and whether a violation has occurred based on those codes and standards.	
Step 3: Identify contributing factors, including one's own belief system, and actions that could have been taken to avoid the scenario.	
Step 4: Select the ethical course of action moving forward, as well as risk factors and continued monitoring needs.	

Scenario 10

George Rastapopoulos has been working with his school psychologists at Rackham ISD to update the department's record retention policies with best practices. In so doing, George has discovered that his predecessors were indefinitely maintaining educational records, with some records being over 50 years old. Given the increased budget this year, George purchased a larger shredder so they can immediately and confidentially destroy all records older than seven years. The destruction of these records will create enough office space to hire two more interns!

Step 1: List all applicable ethics codes and standards.	
Step 2: Describe why those codes and standards apply to the current situation and whether a violation has occurred based on those codes and standards.	
Step 3: Identify contributing factors, including one's own belief system, and actions that could have been taken to avoid the scenario.	
Step 4: Select the ethical course of action moving forward, as well as risk factors and continued monitoring needs.	

Scenario 11

Dr. Jewel Jimenez is a school psychologist working in private practice, who sometimes contracts with schools to complete psychoeducational evaluations. In both her clinical and contract work, she keeps meticulous notes about clients to help her remember the student, as well as to make decisions about diagnoses and recommendations. Dr. Jimenez remembers from her ethics coursework and licensure exam preparation that psychologists can keep notes that are not accessible to others, and so Dr. Jimenez maintains that most of her notes are sole possession notes that she does not have to include in records or allow others to see. Dr. Jimenez keeps most of her notes private and only includes final reports and test protocols in client records, although she uses her notes to help with decision-making frequently.

Step 1: List all applicable ethics codes and standards.	
Step 2: Describe why those codes and standards apply to the current situation and whether a violation has occurred based on those codes and standards.	
Step 3: Identify contributing factors, including one's own belief system, and actions that could have been taken to avoid the scenario.	
Step 4: Select the ethical course of action moving forward, as well as risk factors and continued monitoring needs.	

Scenario 12

Marcia Smith, NCSP believes in the value of strong family, school, and community relations. As such, she routinely attaches copies of student cognitive and achievement protocols to her reports as appendices. She has found this practice greatly increases the understanding of parents and teachers alike when she goes over her report and recommendations. In the rare instances when a parent or teacher questions the scoring of a student's response, Marcia pulls out the test easel and provides a demonstration of the item and how to score it accurately.

Step 1: List all applicable ethics codes and standards.	
Step 2: Describe why those codes and standards apply to the current situation and whether a violation has occurred based on those codes and standards.	
Step 3: Identify contributing factors, including one's own belief system, and actions that could have been taken to avoid the scenario.	
Step 4: Select the ethical course of action moving forward, as well as risk factors and continued monitoring needs.	

Scenario 13

Rubeus Deschain is a conscientious school psychology intern at Gilead ISD. To protect the privacy of those he evaluates, he keeps all electronic records on his encrypted and password protected jump drive. Mr. Deschain even creates separate passwords to open the jump drive, to open the folder containing the files, and to open the individual files. However, he is unsure how to explain to his supervisor that the jump drive no longer works because he accidently left it in his pants, and it went through both the washer and the dryer.

Step 1: List all applicable ethics codes and standards.	
Step 2: Describe why those codes and standards apply to the current situation and whether a violation has occurred based on those codes and standards.	
Step 3: Identify contributing factors, including one's own belief system, and actions that could have been taken to avoid the scenario.	
Step 4: Select the ethical course of action moving forward, as well as risk factors and continued monitoring needs.	

Scenario 14

Susie Hobbes, NCSP was trained to write long, comprehensive reports by the training clinic associated with her school psychology graduate program that resulted in 20–30-page reports. Now that she has graduated and has been working in the field, she has continually refined her reports to make them more concise and increase the likelihood of parents reading her reports. At present, the length of her reports is one double-sided page, with most of the information focusing on developmental history and recommendations.

Step 1: List all applicable ethics codes and standards.	
Step 2: Describe why those codes and standards apply to the current situation and whether a violation has occurred based on those codes and standards.	
Step 3: Identify contributing factors, including one's own belief system, and actions that could have been taken to avoid the scenario.	
Step 4: Select the ethical course of action moving forward, as well as risk factors and continued monitoring needs.	

Scenario 15

Mr. Remus Denton works for a district that has an extreme shortage of school psychologists. They are currently not able to maintain compliance with timelines to keep up with the demand of referrals for special education services and are not fiscally able to contract with independent evaluators. As a solution, school administrators have told Mr. Denton he will need to train a group of select teachers and other employees to administer comprehensive assessments, which he will then score and include in his final reports. While Mr. Denton does not feel completely comfortable with this solution, he does not see any other options.

Step 1: List all applicable ethics codes and standards.	
Step 2: Describe why those codes and standards apply to the current situation and whether a violation has occurred based on those codes and standards.	
Step 3: Identify contributing factors, including one's own belief system, and actions that could have been taken to avoid the scenario.	
Step 4: Select the ethical course of action moving forward, as well as risk factors and continued monitoring needs.	

9 Scenarios for Presenting Credentials and Roles

Introduction

School psychologists often wear many hats and interact with others in consultative, collaborative, and other service provision roles. As discussed in the earlier chapters, school psychologists may also have additional training experiences and certifications, such as psychology licensure or behavior analysis certification. For these reasons, it is important for school psychologists to be truthful about and clarify their roles in professional relationships at the outset of services. Additionally, the terminology used about school psychologist roles may differ from state to state, making it important for you to also be aware of and follow state governing bodies' guidelines on accurate representation and nomenclature. This truthfulness also applies to school psychologists' participation in collaborative relationships, encompassing our disclosure about our roles in collaborative relationships and our responsibility to children and families regarding protection of their rights and welfare.

Guiding Principle III.1 Accurate Representation

School psychologists are ethically required to communicate their "qualifications, competencies, and roles" (NASP, 2020, III.1). This includes being truthful about training and supervised experiences, competence in various skill areas, and roles within professional service provision. Many of you have probably heard the phrase "fake it 'til you make it" in relation to some aspect of your training or practice. While this may be a beneficial perspective when developing self-efficacy and confidence in your abilities, it should not apply to your disclosure of competence when providing, or being asked to provide, a particular service. Instead, school psychologists should indicate their level of competence and any relevant qualifications and seek additional training and supervision when necessary.

This level of truthfulness about qualifications and roles is not limited to clients, but extends to all instances of professional communication, including in public forums. It is also recognized that even when school psychologists are forthright about their qualifications and roles, others may not understand differences between related professions or may misunderstand training and credentialing. A situation the authors have personally experienced and seen presented in public forums, to the extent that it is often seen as a running joke, is school psychologists being confused with school counselors or other related professionals. While this can be a frustrating experience for a school psychologist who wants to be recognized for their own training, credentials, and unique contributions to school communities, it can also, at times, be funny because of the frequency of the mistake. Regardless of your feelings about this situation, school psychologists are ethically

DOI: 10.4324/9781003273950-9

tasked with correcting any misunderstandings of their training, qualifications, and roles. In fact, clarifications should also occur when friends or family members misrepresent you to others. This is especially important when one considers the critical shortage of school psychologists. In part, the shortage may be due to much of the population not knowing school psychologists exist or what they do. For example, one of the authors had an experience when introducing themselves to teachers on a campus they had recently been assigned to where more than a few teachers remarked that they did not even know the district employed school psychologists. Sadly, this is not a unique experience. In addition to the need to correctly represent oneself, school psychologists must also be advocates for themselves and the profession.

While many of the standards within Guiding Principle III.1 (NASP, 2020) are aimed at an individual's responsibility to be truthful in their self-representation, including in the situations outlined, as well as when presenting a current or previous affiliation, some standards also guide one's accuracy in the representation of organizations and programs. For example, graduate program directors must ensure accuracy of information included in program materials, including handbooks and websites. Also of note is that school psychologists are ethically responsible for ensuring any marketing of products or services is accurate. While some school psychologists may have control over their own marketing, such as in the case of a private practice provider, many have limited control over the information that is shared about their services or products. In these instances, school psychologists remain ethically responsible for correcting mistakes in marketing materials and making sure the materials are both truthful and professional.

Guiding Principle III.2 Forthright Explanations of Professional Services, Roles, and Priorities

Guiding Principle III.2 (NASP, 2020) is related to Guiding Principle III.1, as both provide guidance around representing oneself and defining roles; however, Guiding Principle III.2 expands the requirements about being truthful about one's own qualifications and competencies into collaborative relationships. The first standard in this section outlines school psychologists' responsibilities in explaining services to clients and service recipients. Specifically, school psychologists must explain services in a way that is both truthful *and* understandable. Much of the terminology used by school psychologists and in educational settings is not interpretable by those who do not have the same experiences. Think back to your first semester in graduate school. How frequently did you feel like you did not understand what was being discussed in class or by older cohorts because you did not yet know the acronyms (so many acronyms!) or have the same common language as your professors, supervisors, and older peers? Now consider you are a parent whose child is struggling. You want the best for your child and to be involved in their education, but when you speak to education professionals and attend meetings, you struggle with understanding the processes and services. As a school psychologist, we are ethically responsible in this example, and in the many other scenarios where this would apply, to describe the processes and proposed services in a way that the parent understands the information. This is also related to consent, as a parent who does not understand the processes and proposed services cannot provide informed consent for their child to receive those services (see Chapter 4 discussion on Guiding Principle I.1).

A key aspect of school psychology is collaboration and teamwork with other professionals. Many times, these other professionals and teams have the same priorities and goals as we do, but at times, there may be conflicts. Ethically, school psychologists must define their role in any collaborative relationship and respect their colleagues' roles and unique contributions to the relationship. School psychologists contribute to these collaborative relationships, while also promoting the rights and welfare of children. When our goals and priorities differ from others' we must describe our specific roles, priorities, and duties to protect and advocate for children, explicitly communicating our loyalties and priorities. This discussion is recommended to take place at the beginning of the collaborative process, to avoid any confusion and later conflicts related to differences in priorities and loyalties. Often, our duty to protect extends beyond an ethical requirement and into a legal requirement. Therefore, it is important for school psychologists to know not only their ethical responsibilities in advocacy, but also the legal requirements for reporting violations of child welfare. As discussed in previous chapters, advocacy may not always be a comfortable situation. Despite our own comfortability or wariness, school psychologists have an ethical responsibility to prioritize children's and families' wellbeing.

Let's Practice

Below are a set of case studies to help you familiarize yourself with potential ethical dilemmas in the areas of accurate representation and forthright explanation of professional services, roles, and priorities. As always, we recommend completing the scenario worksheets individually and then collaboratively. When working collaboratively, there is opportunity for sharing different perspectives, which may ultimately lead to better problem-solving.

Reference List

National Association of School Psychologists. (2020). *The professional standards of the National Association of School Psychologists.* Retrieved May 1, 2021, from www.nasponline.org/x55315.xml

Practice Scenarios

Scenario 1

Terry Johnson is a school psychologist in a school that has been struggling financially due to budget cuts. The school makes some difficult decisions on which student services to cut back on and which student services are to remain open. The school had been implementing multi-tiered system of support, but now will only be providing core curriculum instruction and required special education services. Tiered intervention services will no longer be available. Mr. Johnson knows this is not in the best interest of students, as many students need tiered intervention supports to be successful, but he agrees to the changes without complaint given the dire financial circumstances of the school.

Step 1: List all applicable ethics codes and standards.	
Step 2: Describe why those codes and standards apply to the current situation and whether a violation has occurred based on those codes and standards.	
Step 3: Identify contributing factors, including one's own belief system, and actions that could have been taken to avoid the scenario.	
Step 4: Select the ethical course of action moving forward, as well as risk factors and continued monitoring needs.	

Scenario 2

Brian McCoy earned an M.A. in School Psychology from an online for-profit university and then took two general psychology massive open online courses (MOOC) that were taught by professors at the University of California at Berkeley. When parents and colleagues ask Mr. McCoy where he attended graduate school, he tells them that he went to Berkeley. Mr. McCoy also has a personal website that he uses to advocate for school systems and to recruit diverse practitioners into the field of school psychology. On the website, he has a biography page where he lists his professional interests in assessment and program evaluation, hobbies such as soccer and golf, and his professional training from Berkeley.

Step 1: List all applicable ethics codes and standards.	
Step 2: Describe why those codes and standards apply to the current situation and whether a violation has occurred based on those codes and standards.	
Step 3: Identify contributing factors, including one's own belief system, and actions that could have been taken to avoid the scenario.	
Step 4: Select the ethical course of action moving forward, as well as risk factors and continued monitoring needs.	

Scenario 3

Ms. Nancy Barkley is a school psychologist who went back to college 12 years ago to earn a doctorate in school psychology. While in the doctoral program, her friends and co-workers began calling her Dr. Barkley even though they knew she was still working on her degree. Ms. Barkley completed all of the coursework, but had twins during internship and was never able to finish her dissertation. After ten years of continuous dissertation enrollment, her advisor informed her that she could no longer register for dissertation and was dismissed from the program because the university does not allow students to be enrolled in a graduate program for more than ten years. At work, Ms. Barkley's colleagues continue to call her Dr. Barkley because she is too embarrassed to tell them that she was never able to finish her dissertation.

Step 1: List all applicable ethics codes and standards.	
Step 2: Describe why those codes and standards apply to the current situation and whether a violation has occurred based on those codes and standards.	
Step 3: Identify contributing factors, including one's own belief system, and actions that could have been taken to avoid the scenario.	
Step 4: Select the ethical course of action moving forward, as well as risk factors and continued monitoring needs.	

Scenario 4

The school psychology program at The University of Educators has maintained NASP approval for over 20 years; however, after their most recent review, the program received a conditional approval status. Given that conditional approval allows graduates the same privileges as full approval, the program director and faculty decide not to update their program website and handbook to specify that their NASP approval is conditional.

Step 1: List all applicable ethics codes and standards.	
Step 2: Describe why those codes and standards apply to the current situation and whether a violation has occurred based on those codes and standards.	
Step 3: Identify contributing factors, including one's own belief system, and actions that could have been taken to avoid the scenario.	
Step 4: Select the ethical course of action moving forward, as well as risk factors and continued monitoring needs.	

Scenario 5

Melanie Carter is a school psychologist who received typical training in assessment, consultation, and intervention. Her training and supervision were weak in the area of counseling. Ms. Carter is tired of doing so much assessment and wants to try to expand her role in her schools. Given the current societal push for mental health services in schools, she sets up a meeting with her administrators to market herself as an expert in mental health and counseling. The administrators agree to split the assessment caseload across several school psychologists and to expand Ms. Carter's counseling caseload.

Step 1: List all applicable ethics codes and standards.	
Step 2: Describe why those codes and standards apply to the current situation and whether a violation has occurred based on those codes and standards.	
Step 3: Identify contributing factors, including one's own belief system, and actions that could have been taken to avoid the scenario.	
Step 4: Select the ethical course of action moving forward, as well as risk factors and continued monitoring needs.	

Scenario 6

Arda Bombadil was a school psychologist for 15 years at Forest Grove Parish before he became the Director of Special Services. In order to keep his school psychology acumen, he periodically completes evaluations himself. Since assuming the new position, Arda has found teachers and principals to be much more receptive of his recommendations. Coincidentally, he has also noticed that when he does unannounced classroom observations the special education teachers have every child's IEP out and are making sure each kid is receiving individualized services as stated in their plans. At times, Arda wonders if the teachers and principals are acting differently because of his new position or if it is because of the new initiatives he has implemented.

Step 1: List all applicable ethics codes and standards.	
Step 2: Describe why those codes and standards apply to the current situation and whether a violation has occurred based on those codes and standards.	
Step 3: Identify contributing factors, including one's own belief system, and actions that could have been taken to avoid the scenario.	
Step 4: Select the ethical course of action moving forward, as well as risk factors and continued monitoring needs.	

Scenario 7

Dr. Liam McQueen recently received approval from his institution to start a school psychology graduate program. In order to aid recruitment for the brand-new program, Dr. McQueen mentions several times on the program website that the program is fully aligned with NASP's Standards for Graduate Preparation of School Psychologists. When interviewing applicants, he is sure to tell them that the program is still collecting data for NASP to review and that everything is in order as the program is fully aligned with NASP standards for program approval.

Step 1: List all applicable ethics codes and standards.	
Step 2: Describe why those codes and standards apply to the current situation and whether a violation has occurred based on those codes and standards.	
Step 3: Identify contributing factors, including one's own belief system, and actions that could have been taken to avoid the scenario.	
Step 4: Select the ethical course of action moving forward, as well as risk factors and continued monitoring needs.	

Scenario 8

Alicia Gutierrez was a school psychologist at Best Elementary School, a renowned school in her area, for one year before she was asked to resign due to not meeting expectations. Alicia resigned and obtained a position in a nearby district the following year. Because her colleagues are unaware of the circumstances of her previous position, she often refers to her time at Best Elementary School to provide credibility to her arguments. For example, when disagreeing with a special education teacher about how to write IEP goals, she argues that "at Best Elementary School, we wrote goals my way."

Step 1: List all applicable ethics codes and standards.	
Step 2: Describe why those codes and standards apply to the current situation and whether a violation has occurred based on those codes and standards.	
Step 3: Identify contributing factors, including one's own belief system, and actions that could have been taken to avoid the scenario.	
Step 4: Select the ethical course of action moving forward, as well as risk factors and continued monitoring needs.	

Scenario 9

Christina Cumby is a second-year graduate student completing her first school psychology practicum. She is careful to sign all of her documents as a school psychology practicum student and always introduces herself as a practicum student. Dr. Paleg is a Special Education Director at Gianna Unified School District. Because the school psychology shortage has gotten so bad, Dr. Paleg has recently started paying practicum students in order to keep them from going to other districts. He hopes this will ultimately result in the practicum students staying in the district after they graduate and become credentialed school psychologists. In order to pay the practicum students, the Department of Human Resources at the district hires the practicum students as Educational Diagnosticians. When Christina attends IEP meetings the principal always introduces and refers to Christina as an intern. Christina does not correct the principal because her major professor has told her not to "make waves" within the district as a practicum student.

Step 1: List all applicable ethics codes and standards.	
Step 2: Describe why those codes and standards apply to the current situation and whether a violation has occurred based on those codes and standards.	
Step 3: Identify contributing factors, including one's own belief system, and actions that could have been taken to avoid the scenario.	
Step 4: Select the ethical course of action moving forward, as well as risk factors and continued monitoring needs.	

Scenario 10

Dr. Reamus Cauthon retired a few years ago but was brought back by Carcassonne Independent School District on a part-time basis to supervise interns and complete contentious assessments. Dr. Cauthon has found that when he uses school psychology jargon, like function of behavior, operational definition, and functional ability the parents ask fewer questions and view him as an expert. Even better, when he uses acronyms such as Glr or ED, he is able to quickly skim through the assessment results, make his recommendation, and return to the golf course. As a younger practitioner he took an inordinate amount of time trying to include all relevant stakeholders in the process, gather input, and provide clear explanations for everything he did so everyone would be on the same page. As a semi-retired professional, he is really enjoying the expert approach to consultation as it is much faster.

Step 1: List all applicable ethics codes and standards.	
Step 2: Describe why those codes and standards apply to the current situation and whether a violation has occurred based on those codes and standards.	
Step 3: Identify contributing factors, including one's own belief system, and actions that could have been taken to avoid the scenario.	
Step 4: Select the ethical course of action moving forward, as well as risk factors and continued monitoring needs.	

Scenario 11

Dakoda Catawnee, NCSP recalls her graduate professors reiterating to her "to always do what is in the best interest of the child." Dakoda is conflicted though because a student recently transferred to her campus that qualifies for an Emotional Disturbance and was previously receiving services in a classroom designed for students with severe behavioral issues. Her district does not have this kind of placement so her principal wants her to qualify the student as having an Other Health Impairment so they can place him in an inclusion classroom. The parents also want the student to no longer be identified as having an Emotional Disturbance as they are afraid it will hurt his chances of joining the military after school. Dakoda is concerned that the student may hurt himself or others if he is placed in an inclusion classroom without a lot of structure. The guidance counselor Dakoda consulted with, Dennis Schroeder, told Dakoda that she is overthinking the whole situation and Dakoda should do what the principal said, or Dakoda is likely to receive a poor evaluation at the end of the year, which will affect her salary. Dennis also expressed support for the principal's desire to reclassify the student as having an Other Health Impairment because he thought it would be easier to get through a manifestation determination hearing and discipline the student for an Other Health Impairment than for an Emotional Disturbance, which he says basically guarantees the student's behavior will be a manifestation of their disability.

Step 1: List all applicable ethics codes and standards.	
Step 2: Describe why those codes and standards apply to the current situation and whether a violation has occurred based on those codes and standards.	
Step 3: Identify contributing factors, including one's own belief system, and actions that could have been taken to avoid the scenario.	
Step 4: Select the ethical course of action moving forward, as well as risk factors and continued monitoring needs.	

Scenario 12

Davis Patterson recently graduated from a school psychology doctoral program and wants to apply to be an NCSP. When he begins completing the application, he notices he did not complete the required 600 hours in a public K-12 school setting. Given that he worked with school-aged children during internship, his program director and internship supervisor agree to sign off on his 600 hours. Davis completes and submits the application and is awarded the NCSP credential.

Step 1: List all applicable ethics codes and standards.	
Step 2: Describe why those codes and standards apply to the current situation and whether a violation has occurred based on those codes and standards.	
Step 3: Identify contributing factors, including one's own belief system, and actions that could have been taken to avoid the scenario.	
Step 4: Select the ethical course of action moving forward, as well as risk factors and continued monitoring needs.	

Scenario 13

Dr. Ellison is a school psychologist who owns a private practice. In their private practice, they do evaluations for families seeking assessment services, as well as for local districts seeking external evaluations. After a recent evaluation procured by a local school, Dr. Ellison's report was not well received by the school. Dr. Ellison's recommendation was that the school should provide accommodations that would be costly. The family agreed, as they had been requesting those services for some time. The school threatened not to contract with Dr. Ellison anymore, as they believed the findings should have been more favorable for the school given that the school paid for the evaluation.

Step 1: List all applicable ethics codes and standards.	
Step 2: Describe why those codes and standards apply to the current situation and whether a violation has occurred based on those codes and standards.	
Step 3: Identify contributing factors, including one's own belief system, and actions that could have been taken to avoid the scenario.	
Step 4: Select the ethical course of action moving forward, as well as risk factors and continued monitoring needs.	

Scenario 14

Viviana Campbell has been a school psychologist for three years. During her first couple of years, she was overwhelmed by her case load and was constantly trying to figure out how her district viewed special education and school psychologists. As a result, she did not volunteer for any additional duties and asked not to be included in school-based teams, such as crisis response teams, counseling teams, or the RTI team. Now that Viviana has a better handle on what she is doing she has more time to devote to these things, but is afraid that if she volunteers for them, she will once again be overworked by her district. So, instead, Viviana hides in her office and pretends to work on reports if someone happens to walk by her office.

Step 1: List all applicable ethics codes and standards.	
Step 2: Describe why those codes and standards apply to the current situation and whether a violation has occurred based on those codes and standards.	
Step 3: Identify contributing factors, including one's own belief system, and actions that could have been taken to avoid the scenario.	
Step 4: Select the ethical course of action moving forward, as well as risk factors and continued monitoring needs.	

Scenario 15

Mrs. Laura Grace just published a book about program evaluation within school systems. She was excited when her granddaughter, Azami, called Laura to tell her she saw an advertisement for the book outside of her college classroom. Mrs. Grace regularly adjuncts for the college, so she is thrilled that the college is supporting her and advertising her academic accomplishments. However, Mrs. Grace is disheartened when Azami tells her that the flyer listed her as Dr. Laura Grace. When she contacts the college to correct the mistake, the college tells her that it would be too expensive to reprint the flyers.

Step 1: List all applicable ethics codes and standards.	
Step 2: Describe why those codes and standards apply to the current situation and whether a violation has occurred based on those codes and standards.	
Step 3: Identify contributing factors, including one's own belief system, and actions that could have been taken to avoid the scenario.	
Step 4: Select the ethical course of action moving forward, as well as risk factors and continued monitoring needs.	

10 Scenarios for Collaborative Work

Introduction

The ethical standards discussed in this chapter involve school psychologists' interactions with others. School psychologists interact with others in their work, whether that is as part of a decision-making team, as a systems-level change agent, to build relationships with community liaisons, or as the service provider within a therapeutic relationship. While school psychologists may be the expert in many of these relationships, we do not know everything. Building relationships with others and respecting the qualifications and contributions of others, even when they are at odds with our own ideas, is integral to our collaborative work.

Guiding Principle III.3 Respecting Other Professionals

Domain 2 of the NASP Practice Model is Consultation and Collaboration, and as noted in the Practice Model, consultation and collaboration are present across all other areas of service delivery (NASP, 2020). School psychologists are typically a part of teams collecting data, making decisions, and providing services and supports to children and families. Guiding Principle III.3, Respecting Other Professionals, highlights the need to work cooperatively with other professionals, provide appropriate referrals when needed, and respect the work products (i.e., reports) of other professionals.

The ability to work cooperatively with other professionals is also related to Domain 7, Family, School, and Community Collaboration, of the NASP Practice Model (NASP, 2020). The ability to build working relationships with other professionals, within schools and within the community, is integral to the work of school psychology. In order to build rapport that is needed to make systems-level changes for the betterment of all, strong working relationships must first be established. In part this can be accomplished by providing quality evidence-based services that are effective; respecting and including other stakeholders in decision-making processes; and notifying stakeholders when changes to services are needed, including the reasons for those changes. Although school psychologists may not always agree with reports from other professionals, including other school psychologists, they honor the professional judgment of the professional and do not modify or alter others' reports in any way, without permission. When supervising a graduate student, school psychologists may alter the supervisees reports; however, the supervisor should be discussing the modifications to the report and the reasons for those modifications with the supervisee to aid in the supervisee's professional development.

DOI: 10.4324/9781003273950-10

Guiding Principle III.4 Integrity in Relationships

School psychologists' work requires the building of professional relationships with colleagues, families, students and children, and other clients and stakeholders. These relationships are incredibly important to our work, as the quality of the relationship is often a leading predictor of successful outcomes across service delivery types. However, it is important to maintain boundaries within those relationships. Guiding Principle III.4, Integrity in Relationships, addresses specific types of relations that are contraindicated for effective service delivery. Engaging in multiple relationships with clients or their family members, whether sexually or otherwise, may negatively impact the professional working relationship that ultimately is not in the best interest of the student. Under such circumstances, school psychologists should ask for reassignment or refer the client to other professionals. However, there may be times when multiple relationships cannot be avoided, such as when you are the only service provider within a rural area. When this is the case, it is the duty of school psychologists to take preventative actions to mitigate the multiple relationships from impeding the quality and scope of service delivery. For example, school psychologists may acknowledge and discuss the nature of the multiple relationships with those involved and set clear professional boundaries on the professional relationship and the types of relationships that are present.

Under no circumstances should school psychologists harass or exploit those they work with, supervise, or recruit as participants in a research study. For example, during graduate training, students may work on research or service projects with faculty. It is important for school psychology trainers to give appropriate credit for any work done by students in order to avoid exploitation due to a power imbalance. Regardless of age of the client/service recipient, school psychologists are not to engage in sexual relationships with anyone they evaluate (e.g., psychoeducational evaluation of a student, evaluation of a supervisee, evaluation of another professional). While many readers may think they would never engage in this type of unethical behavior, the data indicate this particular area of ethics is an uncomfortably frequent violation within the field of psychology.

Let's Practice

Below are a set of case studies to help you familiarize yourself with potential ethical dilemmas in the areas of interacting with other professionals and their respective work products and how to navigate varying types of multiple relationships. As always, we recommend completing the scenario worksheets individually and then collaboratively. When working collaboratively, there is opportunity for sharing different perspectives, which may ultimately lead to better problem-solving.

Reference List

National Association of School Psychologists. (2020). *The professional standards of the National Association of School Psychologists.* Retrieved May 1, 2021, from www.nasponline.org/x55315.xml

Practice Scenarios

Scenario 1

Walter Paddock earned a doctorate in school psychology two years ago and vividly recalls his professor instructing his cohort to only include pertinent information in reports. Given this information he feels compelled to remove information from a report he just received from a school psychologist in a neighboring state. In the developmental history section of the report it states that the student's uncle is a state senator who was arrested for securities fraud. Mr. Paddock believed this information was included for political reasons and does not believe it to be relevant to the provision of special education services to the student so he blacked out the relevant sentences so no one else would be able to see the information.

Step 1: List all applicable ethics codes and standards.	
Step 2: Describe why those codes and standards apply to the current situation and whether a violation has occurred based on those codes and standards.	
Step 3: Identify contributing factors, including one's own belief system, and actions that could have been taken to avoid the scenario.	
Step 4: Select the ethical course of action moving forward, as well as risk factors and continued monitoring needs.	

Scenario 2

Aiden Bukowski was born and raised in the Appalachian Mountains. After earning a degree in school psychology, he returned to his hometown to work at the only school district within 40 minutes of the town. Mr. Bukowski is comfortable working in this district because everyone is related to each other. Given that there are no other school psychologists in the district and that anyone contracted from outside of the region would be ostracized by the community, he believes he is best suited to render services despite the many multiple relationships that exist among students, faculty, and staff. He also assumes that everyone in the district already knows of these pre-existing relationships and are comfortable working together.

Step 1: List all applicable ethics codes and standards.	
Step 2: Describe why those codes and standards apply to the current situation and whether a violation has occurred based on those codes and standards.	
Step 3: Identify contributing factors, including one's own belief system, and actions that could have been taken to avoid the scenario.	
Step 4: Select the ethical course of action moving forward, as well as risk factors and continued monitoring needs.	

Scenario 3

Jessie Hogan is a school psychologist in a rural farming region. She is the only school psychologist for several schools in the area that have formed a co-op for service provision, and there are no other service providers nearby. Because she works and lives in the community, she has personal relationships with many of her students and their families. Parents often stop her to talk about their children at church, the grocery store, and other places in the community. Since she knows many of them have long, busy days working their farms, she does not mind using her personal time to speak with them about their children's schooling.

Step 1: List all applicable ethics codes and standards.	
Step 2: Describe why those codes and standards apply to the current situation and whether a violation has occurred based on those codes and standards.	
Step 3: Identify contributing factors, including one's own belief system, and actions that could have been taken to avoid the scenario.	
Step 4: Select the ethical course of action moving forward, as well as risk factors and continued monitoring needs.	

Scenario 4

Dr. Cannon Landry is a school psychologist working in private practice, providing assessment and counseling services to children and adolescents. His assessment practice has recently increased in demand, and since it is a more lucrative practice, he has decided to transfer his counseling clients to one of the partners in his practice who has agreed to maintain the clients' current appointment schedules. Since the clients will still be attending their counseling sessions at the same time and place, he has the front desk worker notify clients and their families of the change when they come to the office for their next appointment. Many clients feel hurt that Dr. Landry did not tell them beforehand, and they tell the front desk worker that they will be looking for another provider.

Step 1: List all applicable ethics codes and standards.	
Step 2: Describe why those codes and standards apply to the current situation and whether a violation has occurred based on those codes and standards.	
Step 3: Identify contributing factors, including one's own belief system, and actions that could have been taken to avoid the scenario.	
Step 4: Select the ethical course of action moving forward, as well as risk factors and continued monitoring needs.	

Scenario 5

Judy Gonzalez is a school psychologist who has been practicing in her district for the past 25 years. Over the years she has become highly connected to the community and worked with many of the clinicians and community resources available in the area. Dr. Oscar Rubio is a clinical psychologist in the area that many parents take their children to for autism evaluations. Judy has maintained a professional relationship with Oscar over the years but does not respect his work or trust the diagnoses he gives. Dr. Rubio's reports are two pages long and typically include a brief developmental history, cognitive assessment, and an autism rating scale. He does not include observations in a natural setting. Recommendations are almost always for 40 hours of applied behavioral analysis per week in the school setting. As Mrs. Gonzalez nears retirement, she is less concerned with maintaining professional working relationships with providers that she considered to be "bad actors" that appear to be driven by making money and not by helping the child or their family. Now, when parents bring reports from Dr. Rubio to the school, Mrs. Gonzalez treats it as a referral for an evaluation, but does not consider any of the information in the report because she already knows what it will say and does not trust the work of Dr. Rubio.

Step 1: List all applicable ethics codes and standards.	
Step 2: Describe why those codes and standards apply to the current situation and whether a violation has occurred based on those codes and standards.	
Step 3: Identify contributing factors, including one's own belief system, and actions that could have been taken to avoid the scenario.	
Step 4: Select the ethical course of action moving forward, as well as risk factors and continued monitoring needs.	

Scenario 6

Ms. Jasmine Hill is a school psychologist turned Director of Special Education Services. Ms. Hill supports her alma mater by having her school psychologists supervise her alma mater's practicum and intern students. Although she does not personally provide supervision, she does read the reports during meetings she attends and has noticed a concerning and dramatic decline in graduate students' writing ability. Ms. Hill is embarrassed for her alma mater and concerned about the reputation of her own school, so she has mandated that all practicum and intern reports be sent to her two weeks before they are to be presented at any meetings or given to any parents. Ms. Hill takes this time to read and revise the documents to make them comprehensible. Occasionally, she will also add recommendations for interventions she believes would be appropriate based on the information in the report. She then replaces the graduate student's report with her revised report in the student's file.

Step 1: List all applicable ethics codes and standards.	
Step 2: Describe why those codes and standards apply to the current situation and whether a violation has occurred based on those codes and standards.	
Step 3: Identify contributing factors, including one's own belief system, and actions that could have been taken to avoid the scenario.	
Step 4: Select the ethical course of action moving forward, as well as risk factors and continued monitoring needs.	

Scenario 7

Dr. James Tabachnick worked in the schools as a school psychologist for 15 years before transitioning to private practice. Dr. Tabachnick is conflicted about a current client because she has selective mutism. He has no experience with selective mutism and most of the resources he finds online are from the American Speech-Language-Hearing Association (ASHA). ASHA indicates that speech-language pathologists (SLP) are appropriate personnel for treating selective mutism, but the parent reports the school's SLP has refused to even evaluate the child for services, saying it is not something they do. Given the lack of alternative options in the area, Dr. Tabachnick decides to treat the student despite his reservations.

Step 1: List all applicable ethics codes and standards.	
Step 2: Describe why those codes and standards apply to the current situation and whether a violation has occurred based on those codes and standards.	
Step 3: Identify contributing factors, including one's own belief system, and actions that could have been taken to avoid the scenario.	
Step 4: Select the ethical course of action moving forward, as well as risk factors and continued monitoring needs.	

Scenario 8

Jeremiah Twain has been a school psychologist for 17 years. During that time, he has noticed that many non-school service providers, such as counselors and clinical psychologists, do not understand the constraints of school systems and appropriate recommendations for school-based services. Whenever Jeremiah receives requests from parents to work with a student's counselor or psychologist to coordinate services, he attempts to change the parents' minds. He tells them that professionals who do not work in the schools will not be helpful in determining what services their children should be provided. If the parents cannot be persuaded, Jeremiah is standoffish and, at times, rude to the child's other service provider(s) and frequently contradicts their recommendations.

Step 1: List all applicable ethics codes and standards.	
Step 2: Describe why those codes and standards apply to the current situation and whether a violation has occurred based on those codes and standards.	
Step 3: Identify contributing factors, including one's own belief system, and actions that could have been taken to avoid the scenario.	
Step 4: Select the ethical course of action moving forward, as well as risk factors and continued monitoring needs.	

Scenario 9

Julie Ford's best friend has recently taken her son to the doctor, who referred her for an evaluation for autism. She is devastated and unsure what to do, so she reaches out to Mrs. Ford. Mrs. Ford says to let her handle everything. She works in the same district the child attends, so Mrs. Ford knows the process for determining eligibility. Mrs. Ford prepares a letter requesting an evaluation from the school and guides her friend through the process. When the meeting is scheduled, Mrs. Ford's friend requests she attend to speak for her, since the friend does not know much about the process. Mrs. Ford attends the meeting and advocates for her friend's son. The school psychologist at the child's school is concerned about Mrs. Ford's involvement and asks her if she thinks it is possibly a multiple relationship, but Julie says since she does not work at that school campus it is fine.

Step 1: List all applicable ethics codes and standards.	
Step 2: Describe why those codes and standards apply to the current situation and whether a violation has occurred based on those codes and standards.	
Step 3: Identify contributing factors, including one's own belief system, and actions that could have been taken to avoid the scenario.	
Step 4: Select the ethical course of action moving forward, as well as risk factors and continued monitoring needs.	

Scenario 10

Dr. Maggie Turse is a school psychologist with a private practice providing psychoeducational evaluations to children and adolescents. In her practice, she also employs counseling psychologists, behavior analysts, and other service providers so clients and families can receive well-rounded service in their care. One of her clinicians has a child who they suspect has ADHD, and the clinician has asked Dr. Turse to evaluate their child since she is obviously the best person in the area to do the evaluation. Dr. Turse feels a little uncomfortable providing this service to a colleague and friend but ultimately completes the evaluation because she wants to make sure the child receives a high-quality evaluation and because she agrees that anyone else in the area would be less competent.

Step 1: List all applicable ethics codes and standards.	
Step 2: Describe why those codes and standards apply to the current situation and whether a violation has occurred based on those codes and standards.	
Step 3: Identify contributing factors, including one's own belief system, and actions that could have been taken to avoid the scenario.	
Step 4: Select the ethical course of action moving forward, as well as risk factors and continued monitoring needs.	

Scenario 11

Dr. Deacon Duncan is a school psychologist and licensed psychologist who is currently working in private practice. In addition to providing assessment and intervention services, Dr. Duncan provides counseling services to school-age youth. During his last counseling session with a fifth-grade boy experiencing gender-based bullying at school, the client, Viraj, indicated he was seeing the school guidance counselor periodically to discuss many of the same issues he talked with Dr. Duncan about. Dr. Duncan sought permission from Viraj's father to contact the school guidance counselor to encourage the school to immediately stop the counseling sessions as they may be interfering with the counseling services he is already providing.

Step 1: List all applicable ethics codes and standards.	
Step 2: Describe why those codes and standards apply to the current situation and whether a violation has occurred based on those codes and standards.	
Step 3: Identify contributing factors, including one's own belief system, and actions that could have been taken to avoid the scenario.	
Step 4: Select the ethical course of action moving forward, as well as risk factors and continued monitoring needs.	

Scenario 12

Arnaaluk Smitty, NCSP works in a rural community that only has two psychologists who provide services to the community. When making referrals to outside clinics, Ms. Smitty only provides the name of one of the psychologists because she knows and trusts him. Ms. Smitty does not provide the names of both practitioners because she views it as a disservice, especially to people who are new to town and are unfamiliar with the two practitioners' reputations. In Ms. Smitty's opinion, the second psychologist, Dr. Underwood, is racist and often flirts with clients' mothers.

Step 1: List all applicable ethics codes and standards.	
Step 2: Describe why those codes and standards apply to the current situation and whether a violation has occurred based on those codes and standards.	
Step 3: Identify contributing factors, including one's own belief system, and actions that could have been taken to avoid the scenario.	
Step 4: Select the ethical course of action moving forward, as well as risk factors and continued monitoring needs.	

Scenario 13

Brianna Webster has been providing counseling services to Brandy Joyner for the past few years. As with all of the students she counsels, Brianna regularly makes contact with the family to provide updates and gather new information. Over time, Brianna's relationship with Brandy's single-parent father, Moones Joyner, grew closer and more personal. Although Brianna has legitimate feelings for Moones, she also believes the personal relationship that is developing between her and Moones is therapeutic for Brandy as Brandy needs a strong female role model in her life that can help her navigate puberty and show her what a healthy adult relationship should look like.

Step 1: List all applicable ethics codes and standards.	
Step 2: Describe why those codes and standards apply to the current situation and whether a violation has occurred based on those codes and standards.	
Step 3: Identify contributing factors, including one's own belief system, and actions that could have been taken to avoid the scenario.	
Step 4: Select the ethical course of action moving forward, as well as risk factors and continued monitoring needs.	

Scenario 14

Chelsea Bowen is an early career school psychologist who does not feel comfortable providing counseling services to students. Since she does not have anyone to supervise her while she builds her counseling skills and would not have time to add additional responsibilities to her list, anyway, she often refers students and their families to a local counselor. The counselor is a friend of Chelsea's from undergrad, and she likes to help her out with building a client list by referring all students to her.

Step 1: List all applicable ethics codes and standards.	
Step 2: Describe why those codes and standards apply to the current situation and whether a violation has occurred based on those codes and standards.	
Step 3: Identify contributing factors, including one's own belief system, and actions that could have been taken to avoid the scenario.	
Step 4: Select the ethical course of action moving forward, as well as risk factors and continued monitoring needs.	

Scenario 15

Petra Saleh is a school psychology graduate student in her third year. During a summer course, a male professor required students communicate with him via text message. After the course was over, Petra began receiving text messages from the professor. The first text messages were seemingly benign, checking in on her (e.g., "How are you doing?"), but over the last several months, he has sent messages constantly, many asking her to engage in a personal relationship with him and stating that she should be nice to him because he decides her grades in several courses. She ignores his text messages, but he has not stopped messaging her and has begun sending pictures of himself at conferences and on vacation.

Step 1: List all applicable ethics codes and standards.	
Step 2: Describe why those codes and standards apply to the current situation and whether a violation has occurred based on those codes and standards.	
Step 3: Identify contributing factors, including one's own belief system, and actions that could have been taken to avoid the scenario.	
Step 4: Select the ethical course of action moving forward, as well as risk factors and continued monitoring needs.	

11 Scenarios for Self-Interest and Disclosure

Introduction

In this chapter, we will discuss Guiding Principles III.5 and IV.1 of NASP's *Principles for Professional Ethics* (2020), which detail conflicts of interest and our duty to promote healthy environments for students and families. While these may seem like unrelated ethical principles, we hope it is becoming more and more apparent as you further your understanding of the ethics code that many areas of ethical responsibility overlap significantly with other areas. Conflicts of interest, in particular, apply to all other areas of practice, requiring school psychologists to be knowledgeable of their revenue streams, and other benefits, and make conscientious decisions regarding recommendations and referrals, so as not to promote their own success over the welfare of students and families. Additionally, school psychologists, like most people, come into their professional work with a history of learning and belief systems that may, at times, be at odds with their professional responsibilities. A challenge school psychologists may face is balancing their personal beliefs with their ability to engage in ethical and responsible practice as a school psychologist, including at the individual and systems levels of service provision.

Guiding Principle III.5 Conflicts of Interest

The standards under Guiding Principle III.5 (NASP, 2020) can be sorted into three strands: personal and professional conflicts, financial and leadership conflicts, and conflicts when working in multiple settings. School psychologists have professional responsibilities to students, families, and relevant stakeholders, and sometimes those responsibilities will be at odds with our personal beliefs. In these instances, we are ethically required to separate our personal beliefs from our professional requirements and follow best practices and ethical guidelines for service provision. In addition to our beliefs, we must be aware that our actions, even outside of work, may affect our professional reputations and the public confidence in our field. While school psychologists are free to follow personal interests, we must also be aware of the repercussions of our actions on ourselves and the field and do our best to limit or prevent any loss of confidence in our own ability, or the profession's ability, to support students and families. Further, we recognize that life happens outside of our professional responsibilities. Our own trauma, grief, physical and mental disabilities, and other experiences may sometimes require us to pause our service provision, refer certain cases to other professionals, or seek additional supervision or consultation to ensure we are adequately meeting the needs of our school communities.

Sometimes school psychologists' personal interests may lead to leadership or financial opportunities. In these cases, school psychologists must continue to consider and

DOI: 10.4324/9781003273950-11

prioritize their professional responsibilities over personal success. For example, Standard III.5.5 (NASP, 2020) outlines the requirements of NASP leaders, which prohibits any personal or professional conflict of interest which may result in exclusion of leaders from certain activities and limit their participation in decision-making and certain initiatives. NASP leaders, and other school psychologists, must disclose any relevant financial interests when required. This requirement is meant to provide transparency around variables that may affect school psychologists' ability to remain neutral and objective in their professional responsibilities. Further, school psychologists are prohibited from giving or receiving money or other benefits in exchange for referrals or data sharing.

A final potential conflict of interest is when a school psychologist is practicing in both public school and private settings. When working with families and other stakeholders in a private setting, school psychologists must provide information about services available to them within a school setting at no cost. Further, they may not provide services to a student enrolled in their assigned school or district unless those services are not available or offered in the school setting. When working in dual settings, it may be convenient and time efficient to share resources and engage in work for private practice during any "down time" of the public school position, regardless of scheduled hours. Despite this convenience and efficiency, school psychologists may not use any materials or facilities of public school positions for their private practice or engage in private practice during public school contracted hours. School psychologists working in public schools are state or local employees, and their hours and all materials are purchased with public funds. For this reason, the use of these resources is restricted to approved circumstances and activities. Finally, school psychologists working in dual settings may require multiple credentials (e.g., psychology licensure for private practice). School psychologists are ethically required to hold and maintain whatever state-, or other-, required credentials are needed across their settings and provision of services for the duration of their provision of those services.

Guiding Principle IV.1 Promoting Healthy School, Family, and Community Environments

Guiding Principle IV.1 (NASP, 2020) again requires school psychologists to consider variables that may impact student functioning and systems-level support of students and families. Specifically, under this section of the code, school psychologists should actively contribute to creating and maintaining "healthy school, family, and community environments" (NASP, 2020, IV.1). School psychologists are uniquely situated to inform each of these areas of community health and safety, having training and experiences with individual service provision variables, such as child and adolescent development, family systems, school systems, and more. School psychologists are encouraged to utilize their knowledge and expertise in these areas to effect systems-level change. While school psychologists come into a school, district, or organization with foundational knowledge in each of these areas, Standard IV.1.1 (NASP, 2020) directs school psychologists to learn about the specific systems in which they work and to develop partnerships with others that can benefit the students, families, and general school community. Armed with this knowledge and partnerships, school psychologists are then directed to work to promote systems-level change to better serve the school community. This includes, but is not limited to, consultation, collaboration and teamwork, promotion of and assistance with selecting and implementing research- and evidence-based practices, and advocacy on behalf of students, families, and education needs.

Let's Practice

Below are a set of case studies to help you familiarize yourself with potential ethical dilemmas in the areas of avoiding conflicts of interest and promoting healthy environments for students. As always, we recommend completing the scenario worksheets individually and then collaboratively. When working collaboratively, there is opportunity for sharing different perspectives, which may ultimately lead to better problem-solving.

Reference List

National Association of School Psychologists. (2020). *The professional standards of the National Association of School Psychologists*. Retrieved May 1, 2021, from www.nasponline.org/x55315.xml

Practice Scenarios

Scenario 1

Mrs. Harmony Cox is the only school psychologist at Emond's Pond Independent School District. A 12-year-old female, June, sought her services last week for depression because she was being bullied by her classmates and her equestrian coach for "dressing and acting like a boy." After further questioning, Mrs. Cox ascertained that June was in fact lesbian. This information made Mrs. Cox uncomfortable as she was raised as a fundamentalist who believed anything other than heterosexualism was the work of the devil. Mrs. Cox informed June that the teasing comments were actually meant to be helpful, and it would behoove June to start attending church, wearing dresses, and straightening out her life.

Step 1: List all applicable ethics codes and standards.	
Step 2: Describe why those codes and standards apply to the current situation and whether a violation has occurred based on those codes and standards.	
Step 3: Identify contributing factors, including one's own belief system, and actions that could have been taken to avoid the scenario.	
Step 4: Select the ethical course of action moving forward, as well as risk factors and continued monitoring needs.	

Scenario 2

Dee Dee Graham is both a school psychologist in a public school district and a practitioner in a group practice, where she provides psychoeducational evaluations. While she is at her school one day, Ms. Graham's group practice receptionist calls and tells her she has an assessment session scheduled that evening for a client suspected of having autism, but the clinic is out of the autism rating scale she uses. Since Ms. Graham does not have time to order new forms prior to her client session and does not want to cancel the appointment, she takes a rating scale from her school, which she intends to replace once she orders new forms for her group practice.

Step 1: List all applicable ethics codes and standards.	
Step 2: Describe why those codes and standards apply to the current situation and whether a violation has occurred based on those codes and standards.	
Step 3: Identify contributing factors, including one's own belief system, and actions that could have been taken to avoid the scenario.	
Step 4: Select the ethical course of action moving forward, as well as risk factors and continued monitoring needs.	

Scenario 3

Itzel Nguyen travels across the country presenting at state school psychology organization conferences about a new method of determining specific learning disabilities, The Confangled Method (TCM), that requires sophisticated software she created to indicate if a student meets eligibility criteria. Given that she has published a book explaining how to use TCM she always discloses her financial interest in the book at the beginning of her presentations. At the end of her presentations, Dr. Nguyen sells her TCM book and the software to interested individuals.

Step 1: List all applicable ethics codes and standards.	
Step 2: Describe why those codes and standards apply to the current situation and whether a violation has occurred based on those codes and standards.	
Step 3: Identify contributing factors, including one's own belief system, and actions that could have been taken to avoid the scenario.	
Step 4: Select the ethical course of action moving forward, as well as risk factors and continued monitoring needs.	

Scenario 4

Ms. Penelope Finnigan, NCSP receives a request for directory information (e.g., name, address, phone number) and assessment data for all the students she has qualified for special education services due to a learning disability. The request states that the information will be used to contact these individuals' parents to seek informed consent for participating in the norming group of a new method of determining eligibility for a specific learning disability (SLD), The Confangled Method. Although Ms. Finnigan is frustrated with the ever-increasing number of methods available to determine SLD eligibility, she sends the requested information to Itzel Nguyen anyway in hopes that, eventually, one method will once again rule supreme.

Step 1: List all applicable ethics codes and standards.	
Step 2: Describe why those codes and standards apply to the current situation and whether a violation has occurred based on those codes and standards.	
Step 3: Identify contributing factors, including one's own belief system, and actions that could have been taken to avoid the scenario.	
Step 4: Select the ethical course of action moving forward, as well as risk factors and continued monitoring needs.	

Scenario 5

Andrew Benson is a school psychologist who keeps in close contact with his friends from graduate school. One of those friends lives in the same area as Andrew and has their own private practice. When parents ask Andrew for referrals to local practitioners, Andrew always sends them to his friend from graduate school. In return, his friend offers him season tickets to the local professional basketball team games once a month. Since the friend does not give Andrew money in exchange for the referrals, Andrew thinks it is okay to accept the basketball tickets.

Step 1: List all applicable ethics codes and standards.	
Step 2: Describe why those codes and standards apply to the current situation and whether a violation has occurred based on those codes and standards.	
Step 3: Identify contributing factors, including one's own belief system, and actions that could have been taken to avoid the scenario.	
Step 4: Select the ethical course of action moving forward, as well as risk factors and continued monitoring needs.	

Scenario 6

Dr. Harry Baker is self-employed as the only provider of psychological services to a small rural community where virtually everyone knows each other, and gossip travels fast. The town is also known for having more places of worship than businesses. After a contentious divorce two months ago, Dr. Baker began frequenting bars after work and staying until they closed. After the bars close, he makes his way to the strip club that hires many of the local teenagers that dropped out of school.

Step 1: List all applicable ethics codes and standards.	
Step 2: Describe why those codes and standards apply to the current situation and whether a violation has occurred based on those codes and standards.	
Step 3: Identify contributing factors, including one's own belief system, and actions that could have been taken to avoid the scenario.	
Step 4: Select the ethical course of action moving forward, as well as risk factors and continued monitoring needs.	

Scenario 7

In the evening, Dr. Belinda Galadanci evaluates adult clients in a private practice after she finishes work at her school district. Given that the district does not provide Dr. Galadanci with dedicated office space she keeps all assessment kits in her trunk as she drives from campus to campus. To make up for the additional wear and tear on her personal vehicle caused by the added weight of the assessment kits, Dr. Galadanci uses the kits in her private practice, but does purchase and use her own protocols.

Step 1: List all applicable ethics codes and standards.	
Step 2: Describe why those codes and standards apply to the current situation and whether a violation has occurred based on those codes and standards.	
Step 3: Identify contributing factors, including one's own belief system, and actions that could have been taken to avoid the scenario.	
Step 4: Select the ethical course of action moving forward, as well as risk factors and continued monitoring needs.	

Scenario 8

Dr. Becky Forest is both a certified school psychologist and a licensed psychologist in her state. She provides psychoeducational evaluation services through private practice some evenings and weekends in the same region where she is employed as a school psychologist in a public school district. Many of Dr. Forest's clients in private practice are very young children whose parents suspect they have a disability and want to have the evaluation done prior to them going to school. Dr. Forest completes these evaluations without informing parents about their rights and services available to them through the public school system, such as Child Find.

Step 1: List all applicable ethics codes and standards.	
Step 2: Describe why those codes and standards apply to the current situation and whether a violation has occurred based on those codes and standards.	
Step 3: Identify contributing factors, including one's own belief system, and actions that could have been taken to avoid the scenario.	
Step 4: Select the ethical course of action moving forward, as well as risk factors and continued monitoring needs.	

Scenario 9

Amir Hosseini is a school psychologist whose district has recently analyzed discipline referral data and has found that hair and dress code policies differentially affect Black students. As part of the team making decisions based on these data, Amir recommends that, given the frequency of hair and dress code violations occurring across campuses, the district enact harsher consequences for violations.

Step 1: List all applicable ethics codes and standards.	
Step 2: Describe why those codes and standards apply to the current situation and whether a violation has occurred based on those codes and standards.	
Step 3: Identify contributing factors, including one's own belief system, and actions that could have been taken to avoid the scenario.	
Step 4: Select the ethical course of action moving forward, as well as risk factors and continued monitoring needs.	

Scenario 10

Mr. Homer Vozenilek, NCSP, NASP Standards Revision Leader, spearheaded a movement to require an informal self-study of a book he co-authored, NASP's 2020 Standards: What Every School Psychologist Needs to Know Today! as a continuing professional development requirement for individuals' next NCSP renewal cycle. The book explains the changes to the standards and how they impact practice. Most importantly, the text focuses on changes to the ethics code that every school psychologist needs to be aware of and changes to the Practice Model that acts as a service provision guide for practitioners and trainers.

Step 1: List all applicable ethics codes and standards.	
Step 2: Describe why those codes and standards apply to the current situation and whether a violation has occurred based on those codes and standards.	
Step 3: Identify contributing factors, including one's own belief system, and actions that could have been taken to avoid the scenario.	
Step 4: Select the ethical course of action moving forward, as well as risk factors and continued monitoring needs.	

Scenario 11

Dr. Wyatt Cassidy is dually licensed to practice as a school psychologist and to practice as a psychologist. Dr. Cassidy primarily works in his private practice but will also contract with local school districts to assist with the critical shortage of school psychologists. However, the school districts often give him contracts that are well below the minimum hourly rate he could make at his private practice. To account for this, he often gives the bare minimum number of assessments and writes short summary reports when evaluating for a school. He then tells the parents that if they want a thorough evaluation with the full report they should come to his practice for a complete assessment.

Step 1: List all applicable ethics codes and standards.	
Step 2: Describe why those codes and standards apply to the current situation and whether a violation has occurred based on those codes and standards.	
Step 3: Identify contributing factors, including one's own belief system, and actions that could have been taken to avoid the scenario.	
Step 4: Select the ethical course of action moving forward, as well as risk factors and continued monitoring needs.	

Scenario 12

Dr. Omar Gillespie is a member of his state professional organization, so he is apprised of bills that are being considered in his state to limit the rights of transexuals. He is very concerned about these bills, in particular because he works with several transexual students in the large district that employs him. Given the geographic make-up of his district though, Omar believes calling his representative to advocate for transexual youth will be a waste of his time and the representative's time.

Step 1: List all applicable ethics codes and standards.	
Step 2: Describe why those codes and standards apply to the current situation and whether a violation has occurred based on those codes and standards.	
Step 3: Identify contributing factors, including one's own belief system, and actions that could have been taken to avoid the scenario.	
Step 4: Select the ethical course of action moving forward, as well as risk factors and continued monitoring needs.	

Scenario 13

Recently, a publishing company reached out to Ms. Grady about obtaining scored assessment data from students in her district for use in research and product development. Since they are not asking for student names, but rather only demographic characteristics and scores, she does not see any issue with sending the data to them. In return, Ms. Grady receives a $25 gift card for her participation.

Step 1: List all applicable ethics codes and standards.	
Step 2: Describe why those codes and standards apply to the current situation and whether a violation has occurred based on those codes and standards.	
Step 3: Identify contributing factors, including one's own belief system, and actions that could have been taken to avoid the scenario.	
Step 4: Select the ethical course of action moving forward, as well as risk factors and continued monitoring needs.	

Scenario 14

Dr. Ben Stotten holds both school psychologist and licensed psychologist credentials. He is employed part-time in a public school district and is self-employed through a private practice offering student evaluation and advocate services to families in the area. While Dr. Stotten is employed only part-time in his district, the hours of employment and days/times he should be on site are clear in his contract. Despite this, he frequently moves his schedule around to better fit his private practice responsibilities. For a recent case, Dr. Stotten scheduled to meet with the parents of a client to act as a student advocate at an IEP meeting during a time he was scheduled to be working for the school district. His supervisor has called him out on this behavior, but Dr. Stotten believes that since he is providing at least 20 hours per week to the district, that he should be able to complete those hours at any time, despite his contractual obligations.

Step 1: List all applicable ethics codes and standards.	
Step 2: Describe why those codes and standards apply to the current situation and whether a violation has occurred based on those codes and standards.	
Step 3: Identify contributing factors, including one's own belief system, and actions that could have been taken to avoid the scenario.	
Step 4: Select the ethical course of action moving forward, as well as risk factors and continued monitoring needs.	

Scenario 15

Eloise Black is aware of many systems-level issues that grossly impede her school district. However, she is also cognizant of her role and the need to "stay in her lane" so she does not attempt to join committees that set system-wide policies. Mrs. Black is also aware that the district is run on the "good ol' boy network" so there is no use in trying to collaborate with other community providers or even in running for the school board. In short, Eloise is looking forward to retirement in 20 years.

Step 1: List all applicable ethics codes and standards.	
Step 2: Describe why those codes and standards apply to the current situation and whether a violation has occurred based on those codes and standards.	
Step 3: Identify contributing factors, including one's own belief system, and actions that could have been taken to avoid the scenario.	
Step 4: Select the ethical course of action moving forward, as well as risk factors and continued monitoring needs.	

12 Scenarios for Professionalism

Introduction

At a time where funding for education is low and needs for academic, social, emotional, and behavioral services are high, it is imperative that school psychologists represent themselves and the field well. As a primarily publicly funded profession, maintaining public trust and buy-in to our services is necessary for our continued work. As a result, school psychologists should examine closely the ethical standards in the code discussed in this chapter, which primarily provide a basis for maintaining public trust through navigating ethical and legal challenges, self-monitoring and peer mentorship, and contributing to the professional development of new and future school psychologists.

Guiding Principle IV.2 Respect for the Law and the Relationship of Law and Ethics

Being highly familiar with ethical codes, particularly NASP's *Principles for Professional Ethics*, is necessary but not sufficient for the provision of school psychological services. School psychologists must also be well versed in federal, state, and local laws. Furthermore, school psychologists need to know the policies and practices of their employer. At times, workplace polices and even laws may conflict with the *Principles for Professional Ethics.* It is incumbent upon the school psychologist to identify when potential conflicts between ethics, laws, and/or policies are occurring or likely to occur, make the conflict known, and attempt to work collaboratively to resolve the conflict through established policies and procedures. Regardless of the circumstances, school psychologists may not violate basic human rights.

Part of being a school psychologist is being an advocate. As experts on child development, special education law and service provision, and systems-level programs and change, we recognize the many challenges our schools, children and families, and communities face and have a responsibility to advocate for our students' needs to be met. However, when engaging in public speaking, school psychologists must make it known when they are speaking in a professional role as an employee of an organization, as a representative of an association, or as a private citizen. Further, when making public comments, school psychologists should be careful to identify when they are expressing their own thoughts as opposed to when they are expressing an opinion that is evidence-based.

DOI: 10.4324/9781003273950-12

Guiding Principle IV.3 Maintaining Public Trust by Self-Monitoring and Peer Mentoring

One of the many benefits of having a professional code of ethics is that it allows professionals within the field to monitor and regulate themselves (Jacob et al., 2022). If school psychologists did not have an ethical code and mechanisms to address the behavior of school psychologists, then judges and politicians would likely fill this void and create laws with unintended consequences that ultimately do more harm than good because they are not as familiar with the various ways in which school psychologists across contexts and settings may operate as practicing school psychologists are. However, regulation of the field is not the sole responsibility of NASP's Ethical and Professional Practices Board (EPPB). In fact, all school psychologists are expected to attempt an informal resolution with another school psychologist when it becomes known that the other person has violated the ethical code. If attempts to educate and problem solve the ethical infraction have not been resolved in a meaningful way, then additional measures such as contacting supervisors and ethics committees may be warranted. However, there may be times when attempting to address the ethical violation directly with the offending school psychologist is not advised. For example, if you were to discover that another school psychologist had a sexual relationship with a minor student, informal resolution would not be the appropriate course of action. In this case, NASP's EPPB and the local authorities should be informed of the school psychologist's conduct without first attempting an informal resolution with the other professional.

When faced with a troubling ethical dilemma, school psychologists should use an ethical decision-making model, consult with veteran school psychologists, their school psychology state association, or NASP, as appropriate. Both NASP members and Nationally Certified School Psychologists are required to work collaboratively with the EPPB when being investigated. When found to be at fault, school psychologists accept responsibility for their behavior and adhere to the sanctions of the EPPB.

Guiding Principle IV.4 Contributing to the Profession by Mentoring, Teaching, and Supervision

Guiding principle IV.5 Contributing to the Profession by Mentoring, Teaching, and Supervision directs school psychologists to serve as mentors to practitioners with less experience and to graduate students. Even when not engaged in an official mentor role, school psychologists must conduct themselves as role models to others. As discussed in Chapter 2, peer mentorship is an integral part of many school psychology training programs and is now required for school psychologists in their first year as a Nationally Certified School Psychologist. This practice is meant to provide trainees and early career practitioners with social support from those who have more experience. We previously discussed possible benefits of peer mentorship. These benefits are considered great enough that we have an ethical responsibility to mentor, teach, and supervise new and future school psychologists.

As part of this responsibility, as well as personal career goals, some school psychologists may elect to become school psychology trainers. Graduate programs in school psychology, specifically the program directors, have a responsibility to provide accurate information to graduate students and applicants, including the program's current approval or accreditation status. Further, it is the responsibility of field-based supervisors, who cosign practicum and intern student work, to provide supervision to supervisees that is in line with NASP's *Standards for Graduate Preparation of School Psychologists* (NASP, 2020). Furthermore, all the work completed by practicum and intern students is the responsibility of the supervisor. Standard IV.4.2 Graduate Student Supervisors also highlights the importance of practicum and intern students using appropriate titles that signify their role and level of training.

School psychology graduate faculty members and school psychology supervisors are also obligated to adhere to the ethics code and serve as role models by their conduct and provision of mentorship services. Furthermore, supervisors must advocate on behalf of supervisees as it pertains to working conditions and opportunities for professional development. For example, if district administration no longer wants to allocate a minimum of two hours of supervision to an intern because there are too many evaluations and too few school psychologists, the supervisor's responsibility is to advocate on behalf of the supervisee for better working conditions and for an internship that adheres to NASP's standards for graduate preparation.

Let's Practice

Below are a set of case studies to help you familiarize yourself with potential ethical dilemmas in relation to the interplay of law and ethics, application and resolution of ethics, and the advancement of school psychology in a professional manner. As always, we recommend completing the scenario worksheets individually and then collaboratively. When working collaboratively, there is opportunity for sharing different perspectives, which may ultimately lead to better problem-solving.

Reference List

Jacob, S., Decker, D. M., Lugg, E. T., & Diamond, E. (2022). *Ethics and law for school psychologists* (8th ed.). John Wiley & Sons, Inc.

National Association of School Psychologists. (2020). *The professional standards of the National Association of School Psychologists.* Retrieved May 1, 2021, from www.nasponline.org/x55315.xml

Practice Scenarios

Scenario 1

Dr. Hiro Serizawa is the program director for a school psychology program that offers specialist and doctoral degrees. As part of his role as program director, Dr. Serizawa receives several emails and phone calls from prospective students inquiring about the programs. Recently, he has noticed several students asking about the cost-benefit of attending graduate school, given the increasing costs and lack of financial aid options besides loans. Dr. Serizawa informs students that they should primarily consider their desire to be a school psychologist rather than the cost, given that there are several loan forgiveness options available that they would almost certainly qualify for.

Step 1: List all applicable ethics codes and standards.	
Step 2: Describe why those codes and standards apply to the current situation and whether a violation has occurred based on those codes and standards.	
Step 3: Identify contributing factors, including one's own belief system, and actions that could have been taken to avoid the scenario.	
Step 4: Select the ethical course of action moving forward, as well as risk factors and continued monitoring needs.	

Scenario 2

Alise Knight is an early career school psychologist and still feels a little unsettled in her current district. The rest of her school psychologist team has been working together for several years and have great rapport with each other, so she feels a little like the "new kid." Recently, Alise has noticed one of her colleagues often maintains incomplete files, where important documentation is missing. For several of the cases that have been re-assigned to her since she joined the district, the psychoeducational evaluation report is missing or is unfinished, from the students' files. Alise does not feel comfortable bringing this up to her colleague or others, assuming maybe this is just how things are done here.

Step 1: List all applicable ethics codes and standards.	
Step 2: Describe why those codes and standards apply to the current situation and whether a violation has occurred based on those codes and standards.	
Step 3: Identify contributing factors, including one's own belief system, and actions that could have been taken to avoid the scenario.	
Step 4: Select the ethical course of action moving forward, as well as risk factors and continued monitoring needs.	

Scenario 3

Dr. Darius Mooney worked at Tinsel ISD for 32 years before moving to another state to be closer to his grandchildren. His current district has a written policy requiring all school psychologists to use the same report template. Dr. Mooney finds these templates to be formulaic and not as good as the reports he is used to writing, so he ignores the template and writes reports the way he always has. Because Dr. Mooney is well-respected, and his consultation work is highly valued he does not expect much push back from the district. They need him more than he needs them, after all.

Step 1: List all applicable ethics codes and standards.	
Step 2: Describe why those codes and standards apply to the current situation and whether a violation has occurred based on those codes and standards.	
Step 3: Identify contributing factors, including one's own belief system, and actions that could have been taken to avoid the scenario.	
Step 4: Select the ethical course of action moving forward, as well as risk factors and continued monitoring needs.	

Scenario 4

Gwendy, Christine, Dolores, and Gerald are all practicum students at Bless Charter School. They are very grateful for their supervisor, Mrs. Lisey Mercedes, who has always gone the extra mile for them. To honor her, they submitted Lisey Mercedes name to the school psychology state association for a supervisor award. However, they were disheartened when Mrs. Mercedes would not provide them time to attend the state association conference. This was particularly upsetting because they had not been allowed to engage in any professional development while at Bless Charter School. Every time they had requested to attend professional development opportunities, even those provided by the school, they had been told that there were too many kids that needed assessments and the kids should always be their highest priority.

Step 1: List all applicable ethics codes and standards.	
Step 2: Describe why those codes and standards apply to the current situation and whether a violation has occurred based on those codes and standards.	
Step 3: Identify contributing factors, including one's own belief system, and actions that could have been taken to avoid the scenario.	
Step 4: Select the ethical course of action moving forward, as well as risk factors and continued monitoring needs.	

Scenario 5

Annabel Gosse has recently started participating in civil and human rights activism as part of her efforts to improve the lives of her students and their families. Annabel wants to make sure her voice is respected when she takes part in advocacy activities, so she always includes her title and credentials while advocating. Recently, Annabel's school district has started receiving complaints from families and community members with concerns that that district and Annabel, specifically, are not suited to work with their children because of the ideology she is espousing during her advocacy work.

Step 1: List all applicable ethics codes and standards.	
Step 2: Describe why those codes and standards apply to the current situation and whether a violation has occurred based on those codes and standards.	
Step 3: Identify contributing factors, including one's own belief system, and actions that could have been taken to avoid the scenario.	
Step 4: Select the ethical course of action moving forward, as well as risk factors and continued monitoring needs.	

Scenario 6

Ms. Becky Imperioli is the president-elect of her state's school psychology association. As the president-elect of the association, she was invited to be a panelist with other mental health professionals to discuss the needs of children in the modern age. Directly after the presentation, a reporter asks her why parents are becoming physically violent toward each other and referees at school sporting events. Ms. Imperioli replies flippantly that it is the result of two generations of "not enough spanking." The next day, Ms. Imperioli sees no news articles about the prestigious panel assembled to discuss the dire mental health needs of children, but instead, finds a feature article about the school psychology state association advocating for the return of corporal punishment.

Step 1: List all applicable ethics codes and standards.	
Step 2: Describe why those codes and standards apply to the current situation and whether a violation has occurred based on those codes and standards.	
Step 3: Identify contributing factors, including one's own belief system, and actions that could have been taken to avoid the scenario.	
Step 4: Select the ethical course of action moving forward, as well as risk factors and continued monitoring needs.	

Scenario 7

Barbara Walker, NCSP received a Complaint Notification Letter from NASP's Ethics and Professional Practices Board indicating that she was under investigation for possible violation of Standard III.4.3 Harassment and Exploitation. Barbara is extremely distraught because she gave an adolescent male student a ride home in her personal vehicle after finishing an assessment after school hours. The boy's mother could not pick her son up from school because she was recovering from chemotherapy treatments but is now claiming that Barbara had inappropriate sexual contact with her son during the drive home. Panicked, Ms. Walker immediately hires legal counsel to respond to the ethical complaint as she is afraid that anything else she says or does will also be misconstrued.

Step 1: List all applicable ethics codes and standards.	
Step 2: Describe why those codes and standards apply to the current situation and whether a violation has occurred based on those codes and standards.	
Step 3: Identify contributing factors, including one's own belief system, and actions that could have been taken to avoid the scenario.	
Step 4: Select the ethical course of action moving forward, as well as risk factors and continued monitoring needs.	

Scenario 8

Mirinda Seward is a school psychologist who is engaged in human rights activism in her personal life. Her state recently passed a law that requires school professionals inform parents/guardians when a student discloses a non-cis gender identity. Mirinda strongly opposes this law, but given her location, finds it hard to believe the law will change any time soon. Instead of following the law or advocating for its removal, Mirinda maintains confidentiality for all students unless she is concerned about their or others' safety.

Step 1: List all applicable ethics codes and standards.	
Step 2: Describe why those codes and standards apply to the current situation and whether a violation has occurred based on those codes and standards.	
Step 3: Identify contributing factors, including one's own belief system, and actions that could have been taken to avoid the scenario.	
Step 4: Select the ethical course of action moving forward, as well as risk factors and continued monitoring needs.	

Scenario 9

John Alva is a school psychologist who believes psychoeducational evaluation should be left to school-based school psychologists. Over his career, he has encountered several less-than-adequate assessment reports from private practice psychologists in the area. John's experience with these reports is that they only consider data from limited sources, and they usually do not include observations of the child in the school environment. Additionally, John has recently observed a trend where these psychologists are using incredibly outdated measures as part of their assessments. John is so outraged by these continuous occurrences that he begins immediately reporting every psychologist he sees using outdated measures to the state credentialing board.

Step 1: List all applicable ethics codes and standards.	
Step 2: Describe why those codes and standards apply to the current situation and whether a violation has occurred based on those codes and standards.	
Step 3: Identify contributing factors, including one's own belief system, and actions that could have been taken to avoid the scenario.	
Step 4: Select the ethical course of action moving forward, as well as risk factors and continued monitoring needs.	

Scenario 10

Dr. Eddy Matthison is the practicum coordinator in a school psychology specialist program. The program has a standing relationship with a local school district to provide practicum placements for the students. In recent years, several students have complained about a specific supervisor in the district, stating that she is difficult to work with, does not provide constructive feedback, and uses several outdated practices in her own work and expects practicum students to also engage in these practices. Dr. Matthison understands the concerns of her practicum students but thinks having a supervisor like this is good practice for working with other difficult personalities in the future, so she continues to assign students to the supervisor.

Step 1: List all applicable ethics codes and standards.	
Step 2: Describe why those codes and standards apply to the current situation and whether a violation has occurred based on those codes and standards.	
Step 3: Identify contributing factors, including one's own belief system, and actions that could have been taken to avoid the scenario.	
Step 4: Select the ethical course of action moving forward, as well as risk factors and continued monitoring needs.	

Scenario 11

Stephen Collins is a mid-career school psychologist. He considers himself a seasoned pro with a firm grasp on legal and ethical matters. When renewing his NCSP, NASP membership, and state organization membership he always skims over the relevant Principles for Professional Ethics and related state jurisprudence documents to see if anything has changed. When sticky ethical situations arise at work, he already knows what to do because he's been in similar situations before. This gives Mr. Collins confidence to react in the moment to prevent the situation from getting any worse.

Step 1: List all applicable ethics codes and standards.	
Step 2: Describe why those codes and standards apply to the current situation and whether a violation has occurred based on those codes and standards.	
Step 3: Identify contributing factors, including one's own belief system, and actions that could have been taken to avoid the scenario.	
Step 4: Select the ethical course of action moving forward, as well as risk factors and continued monitoring needs.	

Scenario 12

Dr. Anna Camus is the new school psychology program director at Fester University. The program has experienced a high rate of faculty turnover during the last decade and many important records went missing. As a result, the program received NASP-Approval with Conditions status during their last approval cycle. After working diligently to address the concerns noted by the program reviewers and collect all the necessary data, Dr. Camus is 100% certain that the program will receive full approval before the next cohort begins taking classes. Therefore, she informs all prospective students that despite the program's website indicating that the program is approved with conditions, that the program is actually fully approved for the next several years.

Step 1: List all applicable ethics codes and standards.	
Step 2: Describe why those codes and standards apply to the current situation and whether a violation has occurred based on those codes and standards.	
Step 3: Identify contributing factors, including one's own belief system, and actions that could have been taken to avoid the scenario.	
Step 4: Select the ethical course of action moving forward, as well as risk factors and continued monitoring needs.	

Scenario 13

Felix Echeverria recently started his first position as a school psychologist in a large district. He is part of a large team of school psychologists. Recently, Felix saw a psychoeducational evaluation report by another school psychologist on his team where the school psychologist had made several errors, including using the wrong name, at times, and scores in narrative summaries and tables not matching each other. Felix assumes this type of behavior is consistent for the school psychologist and reports them to the state credentialing agency, as well as the team supervisor in their district.

Step 1: List all applicable ethics codes and standards.	
Step 2: Describe why those codes and standards apply to the current situation and whether a violation has occurred based on those codes and standards.	
Step 3: Identify contributing factors, including one's own belief system, and actions that could have been taken to avoid the scenario.	
Step 4: Select the ethical course of action moving forward, as well as risk factors and continued monitoring needs.	

Scenario 14

Edna Ash is a school psychologist in a small district. She has recently taken on a school psychology practicum student from a nearby school psychology program. As part of the practicum experience, the student needs to complete an academic intervention project where they collect baseline and problem analysis data, select and implement an intervention, monitor progress, and complete a report detailing the process with recommendations for ongoing supports for the student. In her school, Edna does not engage in academic consultation or problem-solving, so she refers the practicum student to the instructional coaching team for the project. The practicum student completes the project with the instructional coaching team, and signs off on the final report herself, without any supervision by Edna.

Step 1: List all applicable ethics codes and standards.	
Step 2: Describe why those codes and standards apply to the current situation and whether a violation has occurred based on those codes and standards.	
Step 3: Identify contributing factors, including one's own belief system, and actions that could have been taken to avoid the scenario.	
Step 4: Select the ethical course of action moving forward, as well as risk factors and continued monitoring needs.	

Scenario 15

Mr. J.D. Morton, NCSP takes great pleasure in supervising future school psychologists. He always requests his supervisor assign him two interns so he can give back to the field and do his part to help address the school psychologist shortage. However, this past year he was assigned five interns because one of his colleagues went on maternity leave and another was still recovering from COVID-19 complications. Struggling to keep up with two hours of individual supervision a week, he decided to provide two hours of group supervision instead. Mr. Morton reasoned this would provide a better learning opportunity anyways as interns could learn from each other's experiences and would be more likely to collaborate with each other in the future.

Step 1: List all applicable ethics codes and standards.	
Step 2: Describe why those codes and standards apply to the current situation and whether a violation has occurred based on those codes and standards.	
Step 3: Identify contributing factors, including one's own belief system, and actions that could have been taken to avoid the scenario.	
Step 4: Select the ethical course of action moving forward, as well as risk factors and continued monitoring needs.	

13 Scenarios for Scholarly Activity

Introduction

In this chapter, we discuss school psychologists' ethical responsibility to contribute to the knowledge base of our field. As scientist- or scholar-practitioners, research is at the heart of everything we do and should inform each of our practices. The NASP *Principles for Professional Ethics* (2020) takes this a step further by requiring school psychologists to not only read and apply the findings of research literature, but also to contribute to our knowledge base. Research can often be an area of competency where trainees and practitioners may have less interest; however, the foundations of research methodology and statistics are incredibly applicable to school psychologists' work in practice.

According to the NASP Practice Model, Domain 1 (NASP, 2020), school psychologists are data-based decision-makers who use a problem-solving framework across all areas of service provision, whether that be assessment, intervention, or consultation at the individual and/or systems levels. Trainees are encouraged to make use of the many resources they have available during their training to become proficient in the application of research methods to practice and in the consumption of and contribution to the research literature. School psychologist trainees have access to much research literature through course instruction and readings, as well as university library resources. This is a great time to consume those resources and to get involved with research. For example, students might assist with faculty research or engage in supervised individual research, such as with a thesis or dissertation project. Although peer-reviewed research is not as accessible after graduate school, practitioners can still find a number of journal articles through internet searches and through *School Psychology Review* and other NASP publications, which are available to all NASP members.

GP IV.5 Contributing to the School Psychology Knowledge Base

The NASP *Principles for Professional Ethics* (2020) has ten standards under Guiding Principle IV.5. These standards can be separated into four strands: conducting research, responsibility with research data, publication issues, and reviewer responsibilities. The first strand, conducting research, includes the use of sound procedures and the protection of participant rights. When designing research projects, school psychologists consider variables that affect the internal, external, and social validity of the findings. Further, school psychologists provide adequate information to potential participants and protect the rights of those who consent to participate. This includes disclosing your graduate degree or level of training and following the process of informed consent and

DOI: 10.4324/9781003273950-13

assent. While different fields of study and organizations may differ slightly on the rights and treatment of research participants, all human research must be approved by an Institutional Review Board (IRB) before participant recruitment and study implementation can begin. The IRB process may look a little different across organizations, but each of these processes must meet the minimum requirements set by the U.S. Department of Health and Human Services. Some of the primary purposes of this review and approval process are to ensure that research procedures allow for participants to provide informed consent and assent, and that any risks of harm are minimized and/or are justifiable when compared to the potential benefits. Once approved, researchers must follow the submitted procedures exactly, or submit modifications to the application and await those to be approved before altering procedures.

Once school psychologists begin collecting research data, there are ethical requirements around the treatment and safekeeping of these data. Specifically, school psychologists protect participant data by making sure presentation of data cannot lead to the identification of any participant. This includes research participant data, as well as case study or client data. Further, school psychologists ensure the accuracy of the data that are reported in both research and professional reports. When concerns about the accuracy of the data are brought to the school psychologist's attention, they are ethically obligated to make the data (following de-identification) available for others to review and verify. If errors are discovered, school psychologists make adequate effort to correct the error(s) in any reported findings.

The third strand of standards under Guiding Principle IV.5 (NASP, 2020), publication issues, includes considerations around integrity in publishing, plagiarism, and authorship. Regarding integrity, school psychologists are ethically prohibited from publishing or presenting data that do not make an original contribution to the field. This standard specifically applies to instances of self-plagiarism or other plagiarism, discouraging school psychologists from submitting the same, or similar data to more than one publication outlet or to use others' information or data without permission. Relatedly, school psychologists appropriately cite all sources of information in publications, presentations, and other delivery of information, so as not to plagiarize others' work and contributions to the field. In addition to appropriately crediting external sources of information, school psychologists, when publishing or presenting, appropriately credit those who have contributed to the development of the published or presented work. This includes limiting authorship to only those who have adequately contributed to the project, as well as determining order of authorship. Ethically, authorship decisions should be determined only by the amount of contribution to the project.

Finally, the term peer-reviewed research or literature is often referenced when discussing sources of research information. Peer-reviewed research is typically regarded more highly than work that has not gone through the peer-review process. This is because peer review allows for a sort-of gatekeeping process by which only theoretically and/or methodologically sound research should be published, as a result of peers who were not involved in the project reviewing and providing feedback on a manuscript or proposal of the work. Peer review is typically an unpaid activity in service to the profession and, given that there is potential for conflicts of interest and misuse of unpublished resources, Guiding Principle IV.5 (NASP, 2020) includes ethical guidance for reviewers of manuscripts and proposals. Specifically, although the data and work of the submitters is not yet published, it is their own work and cannot be distributed or plagiarized without permission. When reviewing submissions, reviewers use the materials only for the purpose of their review.

Let's Practice

Below are a set of case studies to help you familiarize yourself with potential ethical dilemmas in relation to research and scholarly activities. As always, we recommend completing the scenario worksheets individually and then collaboratively. When working collaboratively, there is opportunity for sharing different perspectives, which may ultimately lead to better problem-solving.

Reference List

National Association of School Psychologists. (2020). *The professional standards of the National Association of School Psychologists.* Retrieved May 1, 2021, from www.nasponline.org/x55315.xml

Practice Scenarios

Scenario 1

A few years ago, Dr. Tracey Vogel was stressed that she would not be able to meet tenure requirements at her university because the journals she was being published in were not considered "high quality" and because many of her publications were being held up in the review process. To ensure she would still have a job during the first wave of the pandemic, she began enhancing the data in her studies to make them more publishable. After being awarded tenure and promotion, Dr. Vogel felt both emboldened and afraid. She thought the review process was flawed enough that her articles would never be questioned, but also worried that if she were ever asked to make the raw data available to other researchers, she would not be able to without being caught. In an effort to prevent ever having to release the raw data she began publishing articles related to topics that were being debated publicly so she could claim any attempt to verify her results were actually politically motivated attacks and rouse other entities (e.g., politicians, media) to shield her from having to share the data.

Step 1: List all applicable ethics codes and standards.	
Step 2: Describe why those codes and standards apply to the current situation and whether a violation has occurred based on those codes and standards.	
Step 3: Identify contributing factors, including one's own belief system, and actions that could have been taken to avoid the scenario.	
Step 4: Select the ethical course of action moving forward, as well as risk factors and continued monitoring needs.	

Scenario 2

Melissa Benoit, a school psychologist working in a public school district, wants to attend the NASP convention next year; however, her district will only provide professional development travel funding if she is presenting at the convention. She decides she will conduct a survey study in her district to submit for poster consideration. Melissa's idea is to present on educator perspectives of the MTSS that she has had a big part in developing in her district. She wants the data to present the system in a positive light, and so she specifically follows up with teachers she knows love the system to encourage them to complete the survey. Once she has collected the data, she is delighted to find that, overall, educators reported very positive opinions about the system and its effectiveness. Melissa compiles the data into a proposal and submits it for presentation at the NASP convention.

Step 1: List all applicable ethics codes and standards.	
Step 2: Describe why those codes and standards apply to the current situation and whether a violation has occurred based on those codes and standards.	
Step 3: Identify contributing factors, including one's own belief system, and actions that could have been taken to avoid the scenario.	
Step 4: Select the ethical course of action moving forward, as well as risk factors and continued monitoring needs.	

Scenario 3

Craig Kennedy, NCSP works for a school psychology co-operative and provides services to several neighboring school districts. To give back to the profession he cares so much about, Mr. Kennedy began adjunct teaching for a local school psychology program. At the suggestion of a faculty member, Mr. Kennedy partnered with some other school psychology adjunct professors to co-author an article for the state association journal about the benefits of serving as an adjunct and recommendations for how to market oneself to secure an adjunct position. When the article was published, Mr. Kennedy was excited to see that he was the only author listed in the publication because single-author publications would make him more competitive for a full-time faculty position.

Step 1: List all applicable ethics codes and standards.	
Step 2: Describe why those codes and standards apply to the current situation and whether a violation has occurred based on those codes and standards.	
Step 3: Identify contributing factors, including one's own belief system, and actions that could have been taken to avoid the scenario.	
Step 4: Select the ethical course of action moving forward, as well as risk factors and continued monitoring needs.	

Scenario 4

Dr. Kimberly Alves worked as a school psychologist for many years in public school systems before transitioning to working in a private practice. She has now been in private practice for five years but is concerned about retirement. To increase her years of service with the state retirement system she wants to work as a faculty member with a school psychology program within the state. However, she is finding that the job postings are seeking applicants with research experience. In order to make her curriculum vitae more competitive she decides to do research through her practice. After some "water cooler" conversations with colleagues at the office, she begins recruiting participants for a comparative study that will examine the effectiveness of various writing interventions.

Step 1: List all applicable ethics codes and standards.	
Step 2: Describe why those codes and standards apply to the current situation and whether a violation has occurred based on those codes and standards.	
Step 3: Identify contributing factors, including one's own belief system, and actions that could have been taken to avoid the scenario.	
Step 4: Select the ethical course of action moving forward, as well as risk factors and continued monitoring needs.	

Scenario 5

Molly Granger, NCSP went back to school a few years ago to earn a doctorate in school psychology. In her dissertation she recreated a table from a journal article that depicted the differences between major human development theorists (e.g., Bandura, Bronfenbrenner, Erikson, Freud, Piaget, Vygotsky). Given that the table was not directly copy and pasted, her dissertation chair was unaware that the content was derived from another source and complimented her on it.

Step 1: List all applicable ethics codes and standards.	
Step 2: Describe why those codes and standards apply to the current situation and whether a violation has occurred based on those codes and standards.	
Step 3: Identify contributing factors, including one's own belief system, and actions that could have been taken to avoid the scenario.	
Step 4: Select the ethical course of action moving forward, as well as risk factors and continued monitoring needs.	

Scenario 6

David Lestat is interested in the effectiveness of professional development training in his district. He speaks with administration and receives approval to collect survey data and pre- and post-test data for each professional development session offered by the district. He is surprised to find that while educators learn a lot from professional development sessions, based on the pre- and post-test data, they do not use what they have learned in practice, according to the survey data. David is so intrigued by his findings, that he decides to write a research report and submits it for publication; however, he did not receive IRB approval or collect informed consent to participate in research from the educators in his district. He thinks since it was applied research, and the data have already been collected, he will be okay to publish his findings.

Step 1: List all applicable ethics codes and standards.	
Step 2: Describe why those codes and standards apply to the current situation and whether a violation has occurred based on those codes and standards.	
Step 3: Identify contributing factors, including one's own belief system, and actions that could have been taken to avoid the scenario.	
Step 4: Select the ethical course of action moving forward, as well as risk factors and continued monitoring needs.	

Scenario 7

James McPherson is a school psychology graduate student who, under the guidance of his field-based supervisor, designed and implemented a research study on a math fluency intervention. The intervention was successful so Mr. McPherson, after receiving consent from the parents and IRB approval, submitted the data to a regional conference, listing himself as the sole author.

Step 1: List all applicable ethics codes and standards.	
Step 2: Describe why those codes and standards apply to the current situation and whether a violation has occurred based on those codes and standards.	
Step 3: Identify contributing factors, including one's own belief system, and actions that could have been taken to avoid the scenario.	
Step 4: Select the ethical course of action moving forward, as well as risk factors and continued monitoring needs.	

Scenario 8

Javier Ramirez is a school psychologist in a rural school district. He has close connections to the community and is well-respected within the district. During the pandemic, Mr. Ramirez provided several interventions that were required as part of students' IEP. After talking with his former professors, he realizes that because he provided the interventions remotely through teleservices, he should present the data from these interventions at a convention. Given that Mr. Ramirez already received consent through the IEP process to provide the intervention, he goes ahead and submits a de-identified proposal of the data to the National Association of School Psychologists Annual Convention for consideration as a paper presentation.

Step 1: List all applicable ethics codes and standards.	
Step 2: Describe why those codes and standards apply to the current situation and whether a violation has occurred based on those codes and standards.	
Step 3: Identify contributing factors, including one's own belief system, and actions that could have been taken to avoid the scenario.	
Step 4: Select the ethical course of action moving forward, as well as risk factors and continued monitoring needs.	

Scenario 9

Maria Alvarez is a school psychologist who has been asked to be an adjunct instructor for a local school psychology specialist program. This semester, Mx. Alvarez is teaching the program's intelligence assessment course and is so excited to be able to discuss example cases and reports with the students. One of the course assignments is for students to administer a test of cognitive abilities to a child, and then write up the results in a report. Mx. Alvarez provides students with a template and several sample reports. The sample reports are ones Mx. Alvarez wrote as a practicing school psychologist. Ze de-identifies the reports by changing the student names to their initials; however, ze leaves the school's name, teacher name, and date of birth. One of the school psychology students identifies a family friend as one of the students based on the information remaining in the report.

Step 1: List all applicable ethics codes and standards.	
Step 2: Describe why those codes and standards apply to the current situation and whether a violation has occurred based on those codes and standards.	
Step 3: Identify contributing factors, including one's own belief system, and actions that could have been taken to avoid the scenario.	
Step 4: Select the ethical course of action moving forward, as well as risk factors and continued monitoring needs.	

Scenario 10

Justin Graham has been asked to prepare an in-service presentation on crisis response at one of his school buildings. Justin is excited because he has recently completed several professional development webinars on school crisis response and feels prepared to talk about it with others. He prepares his slides using all the new knowledge he has gained but does not take the time to add in citations for the work of others, instead relying only on his memory of the webinars he completed.

Step 1: List all applicable ethics codes and standards.	
Step 2: Describe why those codes and standards apply to the current situation and whether a violation has occurred based on those codes and standards.	
Step 3: Identify contributing factors, including one's own belief system, and actions that could have been taken to avoid the scenario.	
Step 4: Select the ethical course of action moving forward, as well as risk factors and continued monitoring needs.	

Scenario 11

Jeron Lewis has recently been sent invitations to review a few manuscripts that are in his exact area of research interest. He excitedly accepts the invitations to review these manuscripts. While reviewing one of the manuscripts focused on single-case design, he is intrigued by the graphics the authors have created to support their work and thinks they would be excellent resources for students in his practicum course. He saves the graphics and includes them in the resource file for his students. Since the manuscript was reviewed blindly, he does not know who the authors are to cite or gain permission from them. Mr. Lewis tells students he will add that information once the paper is published and he has the author information.

Step 1: List all applicable ethics codes and standards.	
Step 2: Describe why those codes and standards apply to the current situation and whether a violation has occurred based on those codes and standards.	
Step 3: Identify contributing factors, including one's own belief system, and actions that could have been taken to avoid the scenario.	
Step 4: Select the ethical course of action moving forward, as well as risk factors and continued monitoring needs.	

Scenario 12

Dr. Charles Wiley, NCSP regularly reviews convention proposals for the National Association of School Psychologists. When reviewing the proposals, he prints them out to read and then provides a critique of the proposal. After reviewing them, Dr. Wiley saves printouts of the best proposals to give to graduate students as examples of how to write a winning proposal.

Step 1: List all applicable ethics codes and standards.	
Step 2: Describe why those codes and standards apply to the current situation and whether a violation has occurred based on those codes and standards.	
Step 3: Identify contributing factors, including one's own belief system, and actions that could have been taken to avoid the scenario.	
Step 4: Select the ethical course of action moving forward, as well as risk factors and continued monitoring needs.	

Scenario 13

Darius Backmon is a school psychologist completing a research postdoctoral fellowship. While reviewing data for a study before completing statistical analyses, Darius notices there is a lot of missing data in one of the groups. He knows his supervisor will be upset that the team did not collect adequate data, so he utilizes regression information to predict the missing values and includes them in the data set, since he figures those data points will be very close to accurate. Darius analyzes the data, and the team writes and submits the manuscript for publication.

Step 1: List all applicable ethics codes and standards.	
Step 2: Describe why those codes and standards apply to the current situation and whether a violation has occurred based on those codes and standards.	
Step 3: Identify contributing factors, including one's own belief system, and actions that could have been taken to avoid the scenario.	
Step 4: Select the ethical course of action moving forward, as well as risk factors and continued monitoring needs.	

Scenario 14

Dr. Kamal Johansson published a multi-element design showing the effectiveness of a keyboarding program she created in her state association's journal. Excited to be published, but disappointed with the response it garnered, she decided to publish it in a well-respected journal that had a national and international audience. She reasoned that the audiences of the two journals were different enough to justify re-publishing the data.

Step 1: List all applicable ethics codes and standards.	
Step 2: Describe why those codes and standards apply to the current situation and whether a violation has occurred based on those codes and standards.	
Step 3: Identify contributing factors, including one's own belief system, and actions that could have been taken to avoid the scenario.	
Step 4: Select the ethical course of action moving forward, as well as risk factors and continued monitoring needs.	

Scenario 15

Saphira Lightle has recently conducted and published the results of a study examining a math intervention she developed with her research team. The results are making waves in the education field, as the results indicated the intervention was significantly more effective and efficient than the previously most effective interventions. Mrs. Lightle packages the intervention and begins marketing it to schools across the U.S. Some other math intervention researchers are concerned that the results of the study may not have been reported accurately, as the results seem too good to be true based on their understanding of the science of math. This small group requests the original de-identified data from Mrs. Lightle's study, so they can examine it and re-analyze to confirm her findings. Mrs. Lightle rejects their requests, claiming the data contain trade secrets now that she is selling the program to schools.

Step 1: List all applicable ethics codes and standards.	
Step 2: Describe why those codes and standards apply to the current situation and whether a violation has occurred based on those codes and standards.	
Step 3: Identify contributing factors, including one's own belief system, and actions that could have been taken to avoid the scenario.	
Step 4: Select the ethical course of action moving forward, as well as risk factors and continued monitoring needs.	

14 Complex Case Scenarios

Introduction

Throughout practice, school psychologists encounter situations that involve multiple ethical standards. The following set of case scenarios were explicitly designed to target multiple ethical standards. In previous chapters, case scenarios sometimes involved more than one standard but were made to highlight a specific standard within a defined set of standards that corresponded to one of the guiding principles. You now have the opportunity to engage in effortful retrieval and consider all of the NASP ethical standards at once, which may more closely resemble ethical dilemmas you will encounter in practice. Effortful retrieval is a research-based practice in which an individual tries to recall information that has previously been learned. Researchers have shown effortful retrieval to be an effective strategy for learning and retention (Peverly et al., 2014). Thus, we encourage you to try and identify the relevant ethical standards for each case scenario before reviewing NASP's *Principles for Professional Ethics.* If you notice that you did not recall certain sections of the code, spend more time reviewing those standards before working on the next case scenario. As always, we recommend completing the scenario worksheets collaboratively. When working collaboratively, there is opportunity for sharing different perspectives, which may ultimately lead to better problem-solving.

Reference List

Peverly, S. T., Marcelin, G., & Kearn, M. (2014). Interventions for students with lecture note-taking difficulties. In J. T. Mascolo, V. C. Alfonso, & D. P. Flanagan (Eds.), *Essentials of planning, selecting, and tailoring interventions for unique learners* (pp. 387–414). Wiley.

DOI: 10.4324/9781003273950-14

Practice Scenarios

Scenario 1

Michael Armstrong, Ph.D., NCSP lives and works in a very religious frontier area where they do contract work with several school districts in two different states during the day and works as a licensed psychologist in their private clinic from 5:00 to 7:00 pm. During the evening they primarily work with adults, providing parent training services and counseling. On the second Saturday of each month, Dr. Armstrong invites close friends over and everyone wagers on poker games in the normally locked back room of his private office where he keeps clients' files on alphabetized shelves.

Step 1: List all applicable ethics codes and standards.	
Step 2: Describe why those codes and standards apply to the current situation and whether a violation has occurred based on those codes and standards.	
Step 3: Identify contributing factors, including one's own belief system, and actions that could have been taken to avoid the scenario.	
Step 4: Select the ethical course of action moving forward, as well as risk factors and continued monitoring needs.	

Scenario 2

Cindy Mendoza is a school psychology student who has completed all graduate coursework, except for her dissertation. After making several revisions to her study for the university's Institutional Review Board, Cindy began recruiting gay students identified with SLD to her study. Initially she recruited participants by providing flyers to school districts to disseminate, but when she got a low response rate, she began calling the parents of gay children that she had evaluated or worked with as a practicum student and intern. This method was far more productive than her original recruitment plan because she had already established rapport with some of these families. Once informed consent was obtained from the participants' parents, Cindy promptly began the study. After graduating, Cindy published her dissertation study and listed her dissertation chair and her mother, who paid for Cindy's tuition while she completed her dissertation, as co-authors.

Step 1: List all applicable ethics codes and standards.	
Step 2: Describe why those codes and standards apply to the current situation and whether a violation has occurred based on those codes and standards.	
Step 3: Identify contributing factors, including one's own belief system, and actions that could have been taken to avoid the scenario.	
Step 4: Select the ethical course of action moving forward, as well as risk factors and continued monitoring needs.	

Scenario 3

Marty Paulling, NCSP was asked to evaluate a student, Ken, suspected of having an Other Health Impairment due to Attention Deficit/Hyperactivity Disorder. When Mr. Paulling meets with Ken's parents to receive consent, he discovers they only speak Spanish. Trying to be considerate of their time, Mr. Paulling dramatically gestures to where the parents need to sign to provide consent, instead of rescheduling the meeting. As the parents are leaving, the secretary runs up to them with the consent form in Spanish and hands it to them on the way out. When scheduling the cognitive and academic achievement assessment administrations, Mr. Paulling requests the district allow Ken's older brother be present to interpret for him, as needed. Before administering the cognitive assessment, though, Mr. Paulling posts a number of assessment items on social media asking his bilingual friends to verify the way he translated the items into Spanish, using a Spanish-English Dictionary and Google Translate. At the eligibility determination meeting, Mr. Paulling recommends the parents purchase the book Reading to Succeed in Life and Beyond *that informs parents of the importance of reading and about the research related to literacy and financial success. Mr. Paulling enjoys recommending this book to parents because, as a co-author of the book, he receives a percentage from each sale.*

Step 1: List all applicable ethics codes and standards.	
Step 2: Describe why those codes and standards apply to the current situation and whether a violation has occurred based on those codes and standards.	
Step 3: Identify contributing factors, including one's own belief system, and actions that could have been taken to avoid the scenario.	
Step 4: Select the ethical course of action moving forward, as well as risk factors and continued monitoring needs.	

Scenario 4

Xena Carmine has recently received IRB approval from her university to complete a study in a local school district. The school district research committee has approved the study and recommended a campus where the study might be well received. Xena reaches out to the school principal, who likes the study idea so much, they decide they would like to implement it to the entire school. Since the entire school will be participating, Xena does not believe she needs to obtain informed consent from parents/guardians or assent from students. She also realizes she will need several college students to help run the study, since she has many more participants than anticipated. She recruits graduate and undergraduate students in her department to help but provides minimal training since the principal wants to get the study running as quickly as possible. Over the course of the study, Xena observes several mistakes made by research assistants and decides to remove data from the days where she observes errors. Xena also has several students at the school who vocalize that they do not want to participate in the study, but since the entire school is participating, Xena tells them they do not have a choice.

Step 1: List all applicable ethics codes and standards.	
Step 2: Describe why those codes and standards apply to the current situation and whether a violation has occurred based on those codes and standards.	
Step 3: Identify contributing factors, including one's own belief system, and actions that could have been taken to avoid the scenario.	
Step 4: Select the ethical course of action moving forward, as well as risk factors and continued monitoring needs.	

Scenario 5

Ibrahim Gilbert has been a school psychologist for 30 years, and has seen many changes in policy, law, and professional ethics during that time. As he comes closer to retirement, Ibrahim believes there is no need to remain up to date on new legislation and policies, as he assumes his district will likely notify him if something major changes. Given that he will not need to renew his credential prior to his planned retirement, he has also stopped completing professional development and continuing education, instead completing his work just as he always has. When his intern asks him about recent changes, Ibrahim tells the intern to "do whatever your graduate program told you to do."

Step 1: List all applicable ethics codes and standards.	
Step 2: Describe why those codes and standards apply to the current situation and whether a violation has occurred based on those codes and standards.	
Step 3: Identify contributing factors, including one's own belief system, and actions that could have been taken to avoid the scenario.	
Step 4: Select the ethical course of action moving forward, as well as risk factors and continued monitoring needs.	

Scenario 6

Damon Udri, Ph.D. is dually licensed as a school psychologist and as a psychologist. Five years ago, Dr. Udri began working in a hospital. Since beginning work at the hospital, Dr. Udri has exclusively focused his professional development on the effects of rare genetic disorders on children. At first, he did this to get up to speed on his new position as quickly as possible but then continued attending these sessions out of inertia. One of his favorite things about working at the hospital is that that he has access to expensive assessment and report writing software that will both score his assessments and produce a report with his digital signature attached. This is a huge time saver as he can just print the report and give it to an intern to explain to the parents. In fact, his work-life balance has never been better!

Step 1: List all applicable ethics codes and standards.	
Step 2: Describe why those codes and standards apply to the current situation and whether a violation has occurred based on those codes and standards.	
Step 3: Identify contributing factors, including one's own belief system, and actions that could have been taken to avoid the scenario.	
Step 4: Select the ethical course of action moving forward, as well as risk factors and continued monitoring needs.	

Scenario 7

Lydia Rhodes is in her 5th year as a school psychologist. She struggles with developing behavior intervention plans from functional behavior assessment data. In particular, she has a hard time developing functional hypotheses through problem-solving and identifying effective recommendations. Ms. Rhodes knows she should attend continuing education training and ask for supervision to complete these tasks with competence, but she just does not have the time to do more training since her caseload is so high. Instead, she often makes recommendations for behavior plans based on the topography of the behavior, rather than through a problem-solving process that is individualized for each student. Ms. Rhodes thinks her recommendations are effective most of the time, but sometimes student behavior worsens after her recommendations are implemented.

Step 1: List all applicable ethics codes and standards.	
Step 2: Describe why those codes and standards apply to the current situation and whether a violation has occurred based on those codes and standards.	
Step 3: Identify contributing factors, including one's own belief system, and actions that could have been taken to avoid the scenario.	
Step 4: Select the ethical course of action moving forward, as well as risk factors and continued monitoring needs.	

Scenario 8

Mariah Deeson has recently taken on a position in a new district. She made this change because her previous position required her to do a significant amount of academic and behavioral consultation, and she prefers assessment practices. Recently, her new district has been considering building MTSS in their schools and asked Mariah to be involved in the process of setting up policies and procedures related to this venture. Mariah tells them she would prefer not to be involved and to just complete assessments for students referred for special education services, as she does not see the benefit of MTSS. Coincidentally, she despised the professor that taught MTSS in graduate school. Additionally, Mariah begins telling teachers and other staff that MTSS are not effective in her experience, and that they should fight against using limited school resources for these programs.

Step 1: List all applicable ethics codes and standards.	
Step 2: Describe why those codes and standards apply to the current situation and whether a violation has occurred based on those codes and standards.	
Step 3: Identify contributing factors, including one's own belief system, and actions that could have been taken to avoid the scenario.	
Step 4: Select the ethical course of action moving forward, as well as risk factors and continued monitoring needs.	

Scenario 9

Dr. Amelia McKie is a school psychologist working in private practice providing psychoeducational assessments to children in the community. As part of the practice, Dr. McKie has an office manager, who answers the office phone and email account, greets clients, and completes billing forms. Dr. McKie hired the current office manager, knowing they had significant experience working in other psychology practices. Therefore, Dr. McKie did not provide comprehensive ethical training. Dr. McKie is very busy, and so she also has the office manager complete all client intake meetings given her previous experience in clinical settings. This includes providing an overview of services, collecting data about the reason for seeking services, and reviewing and gaining informed consent. Although Dr. McKie provided training to the office manager on each part of the intake meeting, she discovers the office manager is only having the clients sign informed consent, rather than reviewing and gaining true informed consent for services. It also comes to Dr. McKie's attention that the office manager has been discussing clients with a practicum student in the waiting room while other clients are present.

Step 1: List all applicable ethics codes and standards.	
Step 2: Describe why those codes and standards apply to the current situation and whether a violation has occurred based on those codes and standards.	
Step 3: Identify contributing factors, including one's own belief system, and actions that could have been taken to avoid the scenario.	
Step 4: Select the ethical course of action moving forward, as well as risk factors and continued monitoring needs.	

Scenario 10

Kazi Pierite is a 14-year-old student at Hightower High School, who asked the school psychologist, Ms. Lacy, for assistance with virtual bullying he is receiving from classmates and neighbors. Ms. Lacy agrees to counsel Kazi without telling Kazi's parents because Kazi is afraid if his parents know they will limit his access to electronics. After two years of working privately together, Ms. Lacy and Kazi develop a sexual relationship.

Step 1: List all applicable ethics codes and standards.	
Step 2: Describe why those codes and standards apply to the current situation and whether a violation has occurred based on those codes and standards.	
Step 3: Identify contributing factors, including one's own belief system, and actions that could have been taken to avoid the scenario.	
Step 4: Select the ethical course of action moving forward, as well as risk factors and continued monitoring needs.	

Scenario 11

Wilhelmina Lodewijk, NCSP received permission from the parents of an 8-year-old boy, Patrick, to evaluate him for special education services. Patrick's mother is the local mayor, and his father is the pastor of a megachurch. After completing a direct observation, cognitive assessment, and teacher interviews, the parents informed Ms. Lodewijk they no longer wanted Patrick evaluated for special education services, preferring instead to seek private services. Ms. Lodewijk, being a seasoned professional, assumed the parents would return for a full evaluation within a few years so she went ahead and completed an academic assessment, wrote a summary report, and placed it in Patrick's file. Given the high-profile status of Patrick's parents, Ms. Lodewijk was frequently approached by teachers wanting to know the results of the evaluation. Because Ms. Lodewijk was resentful the evaluation was terminated prematurely, which she believed was not in the best interest of the child, and because she disagreed with the political affiliation of both parents, she informed any teacher that asked about the results of the evaluation.

Step 1: List all applicable ethics codes and standards.	
Step 2: Describe why those codes and standards apply to the current situation and whether a violation has occurred based on those codes and standards.	
Step 3: Identify contributing factors, including one's own belief system, and actions that could have been taken to avoid the scenario.	
Step 4: Select the ethical course of action moving forward, as well as risk factors and continued monitoring needs.	

Scenario 12

Jim Heggy, NCSP is an early career professional working at a private school in a suburban area. Many of the students at the private school display severe symptoms of anxiety, so Mr. Heggy only makes notations on assessment protocols when students answer correctly. However, Mr. Heggy has been finding that much of the students' anxiety is a result of demanding, well-to-do parents. In response, he has started a Grit Group at the school for anxious students. During group sessions, Mr. Heggy tells them social stories of students who he considers to face real problems, such as only having one meal a day, walking home in unsafe neighborhoods, and playing with needles found at the local park. When parents ask him what their children do during the group counseling sessions, Mr. Heggy explains to them that they are working on developing grit as defined by Dr. Angela Duckworth and provides them with journal articles by Dr. Duckworth if they ask additional questions.

Step 1: List all applicable ethics codes and standards.	
Step 2: Describe why those codes and standards apply to the current situation and whether a violation has occurred based on those codes and standards.	
Step 3: Identify contributing factors, including one's own belief system, and actions that could have been taken to avoid the scenario.	
Step 4: Select the ethical course of action moving forward, as well as risk factors and continued monitoring needs.	

Scenario 13

Elroy Logan is a school psychologist working in a rural area. He is a deeply religious man who believes in an abstinence-only approach to sex education and that premarital sex is an abomination. With increasing frequency, Mr. Logan has received special education referrals for students who are pregnant. Based on his belief system, he provides a perfunctory evaluation and identifies them as having an emotional disturbance. When providing counseling services to these young women, Mr. Logan spends a great deal of time convincing the female students they need to marry their baby's father and that in so doing, they will free themselves from their mental disturbances.

Step 1: List all applicable ethics codes and standards.	
Step 2: Describe why those codes and standards apply to the current situation and whether a violation has occurred based on those codes and standards.	
Step 3: Identify contributing factors, including one's own belief system, and actions that could have been taken to avoid the scenario.	
Step 4: Select the ethical course of action moving forward, as well as risk factors and continued monitoring needs.	

Scenario 14

Mindy Li graduated from a school psychology program with a heavy emphasis in behaviorism. As a first-year school psychologist, she realized her colleagues expected her to give the Rorschach and sentence completion tests to determine eligibility for Emotional Disturbance. After receiving a template for how to write these tests in her report, she began administering and using the tests to determine eligibility as well. When contacted by NASP's EPPB to investigate a complaint about her provision of services, she immediately hired a parent of a student she is currently evaluating for autism to respond to the EPPB. Mrs. Li chose this parent to represent her because he is a high-profile lawyer.

Step 1: List all applicable ethics codes and standards.	
Step 2: Describe why those codes and standards apply to the current situation and whether a violation has occurred based on those codes and standards.	
Step 3: Identify contributing factors, including one's own belief system, and actions that could have been taken to avoid the scenario.	
Step 4: Select the ethical course of action moving forward, as well as risk factors and continued monitoring needs.	

Scenario 15

Ms. Maude Simpson has recently moved to a new state and started a job as a school psychologist after practicing in another state for ten years. Ismael, a tenth-grade student, requests counseling services from her. Ismael reports feelings of intense anxiety throughout the day and has a diagnosis of Generalized Anxiety Disorder, given by their primary care physician, and takes daily medication to treat anxiety. The student does not receive any special education services or accommodation at school. In Ms. Simpson's previous state, mature minors could request and receive school psychological services without parental consent. Given Ismael is 16 years old, Ms. Simpson determines Ismael is mature enough to seek services without parental consent and agrees to provide counseling services. After six weeks of providing counseling services to Ismael, Ms. Simpson receives an angry call from Ismael's father. He is upset that he was not notified of the provision of services to Ismael and that he did not consent to them. Ms. Simpson learns through this phone call that her current state law does not allow her to provide psychological services to mature minors without parental consent. Ms. Simpson decides to stop providing services to Ismael without providing a rationale to the parents for continuing, given that the father has stated he will not consent to these services.

Step 1: List all applicable ethics codes and standards.	
Step 2: Describe why those codes and standards apply to the current situation and whether a violation has occurred based on those codes and standards.	
Step 3: Identify contributing factors, including one's own belief system, and actions that could have been taken to avoid the scenario.	
Step 4: Select the ethical course of action moving forward, as well as risk factors and continued monitoring needs.	

Appendix A
Reproducible Ethical Decision-Making Model Form

Step 1: List all applicable ethics codes and standards.	
Step 2: Describe why those codes and standards apply to the current situation and whether a violation has occurred based on those codes and standards.	
Step 3: Identify contributing factors, including one's own belief system, and actions that could have been taken to avoid the scenario.	
Step 4: Select the ethical course of action moving forward, as well as risk factors and continued monitoring needs.	

Appendix B

National Association of School Psychologists Principles for Professional Ethics 2020

Principles for Professional Ethics

PURPOSE

The formal principles that elucidate the proper conduct of a professional school psychologist are known as ethics. In 1974, NASP adopted its first code of ethics, the *Principles for Professional Ethics* (Principles), and revisions were made in 1984, 1992, 1997, 2000, and 2010. The purpose of the Principles is to protect the public and those who receive school psychological services by sensitizing school psychologists to the ethical aspects of their work, educating them about appropriate conduct, helping them monitor their own behavior, and providing standards to be used in the resolution of complaints of unethical conduct. NASP members and school psychologists who are certified by the National School Psychology Certification System (i.e., those who hold the Nationally Certified School Psychologist credential, NCSP) are bound to abide by NASP's code of ethics.

The NASP *Principles for Professional Ethics* were developed to address the unique circumstances associated with providing school psychological services.[1] The duty to educate children and youth and the legal authority to do so rest with state governments. When school psychologists employed by school boards make decisions in their official roles, such acts are seen as actions by state government. As state actors, school-based practitioners have special obligations to all students. They must know and respect the rights of students under the U.S. Constitution and federal and state statutory law. They must balance the authority of parents to make decisions about their children with the needs and rights of those children, and with the purposes and authority of schools. Furthermore, as school employees, school psychologists have a legal as well as an ethical obligation to take steps to protect all students from reasonably foreseeable risk of harm. Finally, school-based practitioners work in a context that emphasizes multidisciplinary problem solving and intervention. For these reasons, psychologists employed by the schools may have less control over aspects of service delivery than practitioners in private practice. However, within this framework, it is expected that school psychologists will make careful, reasoned, and principled ethical choices based on knowledge of this code, recognizing that responsibility for ethical conduct rests with the individual practitioner.

School psychologists are committed to the application of their professional expertise for the purpose of promoting improvement in the quality of life for students, families, and school communities. This objective is pursued in ways that protect the dignity and rights of those involved. School psychologists consider the interests and rights of children and youth to be their highest priority in decision making, and act as advocates for all students. These assumptions necessitate that school psychologists speak up for the needs and rights of students even when it may be difficult to do so.

[1] The National Association of School Psychologists wishes to acknowledge prior work by the American Psychological Association and the Canadian Psychological Association as sources for some of these themes, principles, and standards.

USING THE NASP ETHICAL PRINCIPLES

The *Principles for Professional Ethics*, like all codes of ethics, provides only limited guidance in making ethical choices. Individual judgment is necessary to apply the code to situations that arise in professional practice. Ethical dilemmas may be created by situations involving competing ethical principles, conflicts between ethics and law, the conflicting interests of multiple parties, the dual roles as employee and pupil advocate, or because it is difficult to decide how statements in the ethics code apply to a particular situation. Such situations are often complicated and may require a nuanced application of these Principles to affect a resolution that results in the greatest benefit for the student and concerned others. When difficult situations arise, school psychologists are advised to use a systematic problem-solving process to identify the best course of action. This process should include identifying the ethical issues involved, consulting these Principles, consulting colleagues with greater expertise, evaluating the rights and welfare of all affected parties, considering alternative solutions and their consequences, and accepting responsibility for the decisions made.

The NASP *Principles for Professional Ethics* may require a more stringent standard of conduct than law, and in those situations in which both apply, school psychologists are expected to adhere to the Principles. For example, federal special education law generally requires parental notice of their legal rights in the school setting, a signed consent form for an evaluation by a school psychologist, and an invitation to parents to participate in meetings when important school decisions are being made about their child. In contrast, school psychologists have more comprehensive ethical requirements when working with parents. School psychologists are ethically obligated to ensure that parents understand their legal rights; understand what it is they are consenting, or refusing to consent, to; and understand the implications of that decision. In addition, school psychologists are ethically required to ensure that parents are afforded the opportunity to meaningfully participate in important decisions affecting their own child.

When conflicts between ethics and law occur, school psychologists are expected to take steps to resolve conflicts in a problem-solving process with others and through positive, respected, and legal channels. If they are not able to resolve the conflict in this manner, they may abide by the law, as long as the resulting actions do not violate basic human rights. If law or district policy poses a barrier to ethical practice, school psychologists must advocate for changes in those laws or policies and practices to better align them with ethical standards.

The *Principles for Professional Ethics* provides standards for professional conduct. School psychologists, in their private lives, are free to pursue their personal interests, except to the degree that those interests compromise trust in the profession or professional effectiveness. The boundary between professional and personal behaviors is not clear-cut, however, particularly in venues such as social media. Furthermore, school professionals are held to a higher standard of good character and conduct than others because they serve as role models for children. For these reasons, school psychologists are encouraged to avoid actions that are disrespectful of the dignity of others and that could negatively affect their credibility and diminish trust in the profession.

School psychologists practice in a variety of settings, including public and private schools, juvenile justice institutions, colleges and universities, mental health clinics, hospitals, and private practice. In addition, school psychologists may be employed as practitioners or in a variety of roles, including administration and supervision. The principles in this code should be considered by school psychologists in their ethical decision making regardless of their role and employment setting. However, this revision of the code, like its precursors, focuses on the special challenges associated with providing school psychological services within schools and to students. School psychologists who provide services directly to children, parents, and other clients as private practitioners, and those who work in health and mental health settings, are encouraged to be knowledgeable of federal and state laws regulating mental health providers, and to consult the American Psychological Association's (2017) *Ethical Principles of Psychologists and Code of Conduct* for guidance on issues not directly addressed in this code.

Four broad ethical themes provide the organizational framework for the 2020 *Principles for Professional Ethics.* Each of the four broad themes are aspirational and identify fundamental principles that underlie the ethical practice of school psychology. Each ethical theme subsumes guiding principles that help explain ways in which broad ethical principles apply to professional practice. Guiding principles are to be considered in ethical decision making. However, because their purpose is to identify ethical considerations associated with practice situations, the guiding principles are aspirational rather than enforceable. The guiding principles are further articulated by multiple specific enforceable standards of conduct. As much as feasible, the enforceable standards identify actions (or failures to act) that the profession considers ethical or unethical conduct. NASP will seek to enforce the ethical standards for specific professional conduct in accordance with NASP's Ethics and Professional Practices Board Procedures. Regardless of role, clientele, or setting, school psychologists should reflect on the theme and intent of each ethical principle and standard to determine their application to individual situations.

School psychologists are helping professionals. Their decisions, including to act or the failure to act, affect the welfare of children and families. In their professional roles, school psychologists have a duty not only to avoid ethics code violations but also to take affirmative steps to benefit clients, schools, families, and the community. For this reason, school psychologists are encouraged to strive for excellence rather than simply meeting the minimum obligations outlined in the *Principles for Professional Ethics*, and to engage in the lifelong learning that is necessary to achieve and maintain expertise in applied professional ethics.

DEFINITION OF TERMS AS USED IN THE PRINCIPLES FOR PROFESSIONAL ETHICS

Client: The *client* is the person or persons with whom the school psychologist establishes a professional relationship for the purpose of providing school psychological services. A school psychologist–client professional relationship is established by an informed agreement with client(s) about the school psychologist's ethical and other duties to each party. While not clients per se, classrooms, schools, school systems, families, and communities also may be recipients of school psychological services and often are parties with an interest in the actions of school psychologists.

Child: In law, the term *child* generally refers to a minor, a person younger than the age of majority. *Child* is used in this document to indicate minor status or the parent–child relationship. The term *student* refers to a child, youth, or adult enrolled in an educational setting.

Informed consent: Informed consent means that the person giving consent has the legal authority to make a consent decision and a clear understanding of what it is they are consenting to, and that their consent is freely given and may be withdrawn without prejudice.

Assent: The term *assent* refers to a minor's affirmative agreement to participate in psychological services or research.

Parent: The term *parent* may be defined in law or district policy, and can include the birth or adoptive parent, an individual acting in the place of a natural or adoptive parent (a grandparent or other relative, stepparent, or domestic partner), and/or an individual who is legally responsible for the child's welfare.

Advocacy: School psychologists have a special obligation to speak up for the rights and welfare of students and families, and to provide a voice to clients who cannot or do not wish to speak for themselves. Advocacy also occurs when school psychologists use their expertise in psychology and education to promote changes in schools, systems, and laws that will benefit schoolchildren, other students, and families. Nothing in this code of ethics, however, should be construed as requiring school psychologists to engage in insubordination (defined as the willful disregard of an employer's lawful instructions) or to file a complaint about school district practices with a federal or state regulatory agency as part of their advocacy efforts.

School-based versus private practice: For the purposes of this document, *school-based practice* refers to the provision of school psychological services under the authority of a state, regional, or local educational agency. School-based practice occurs if the school psychologist is an employee of the schools or is contracted by the schools on a case or consultative basis. *Private practice* occurs when a school psychologist enters into an agreement with a client rather than an educational agency to provide school psychological services and when the school psychologist's fee for services is the responsibility of the client or their representative.

BROAD THEME I. RESPECTING THE DIGNITY AND RIGHTS OF ALL PERSONS

School psychologists engage only in professional practices that maintain the dignity of all with whom they work. In their words and actions, school psychologists demonstrate respect for the autonomy of persons and their right to self-determination, respect for privacy, and a commitment to just, equitable, and fair treatment of all persons.

GUIDING PRINCIPLE I.1 AUTONOMY AND SELF-DETERMINATION

School psychologists respect the right of persons to participate in decisions affecting their own welfare. (See *informed consent* in the Definition of Terms.) They recognize that informed consent is an ongoing process, and they reopen discussion of consent when appropriate, such as when there is a significant change in previously agreed upon goals and services, or when decisions must be made regarding the sharing of sensitive information with others.

Standard I.1.1 When Consent Is/Is Not Required

School psychologists encourage and promote parental participation in school decisions affecting their children. However, where school psychologists are members of the school's educational support staff, not all of their services require informed parental consent. It is ethically permissible to provide school-based consultation services regarding a child or adolescent to a student assistance team or teacher without informed parental consent as long as the resulting interventions are under the authority of the teacher and within the scope of typical classroom interventions. Parental consent is not ethically required for a school-based school psychologist to review a student's education records, conduct classroom observations, assist in within-classroom interventions and progress monitoring, or participate in educational screenings conducted as part of a regular program of instruction. Parental consent is required if the consultation about a particular child or adolescent is likely to be extensive and ongoing and/or if school actions may result in a significant intrusion on student or family privacy beyond what might be expected in the course of ordinary school activities. Parents must be notified when the school or school psychologist intends to administer to students a survey that screens for mental health problems, and those parents must be given the opportunity to remove their child or adolescent from participation in such screenings.

Standard I.1.2 Consent to Establish a School Psychologist–Client Relationship

Except for urgent situations or self-referrals by a minor student, school psychologists seek parental consent (or the consent of an adult student) prior to establishing a school psychologist–client relationship for the purpose of psychological diagnosis, assessment of eligibility for special education or disability accommodations, or to provide ongoing individual or group counseling, or other therapeutic intervention outside the classroom. (See *informed consent* in the Definition of Terms.)

I.1.2a It is ethically permissible to provide psychological assistance without parental notice or consent in emergency situations or if there is reason to believe a student may pose a danger to others; is at risk for self-harm; or is in danger of injury, exploitation, or maltreatment.

I.1.2b When a student who is a minor self-refers for assistance, it is ethically permissible to provide psychological assistance without parental notice or consent for one or several meetings to establish the nature and degree of the need for services and to ensure that the child is safe and not in danger. It is ethically permissible to provide services to mature minors without parental consent where allowed by state law and school district policy. However, if the student is not old enough to receive school psychological assistance independent of parental consent, the school psychologist obtains parental consent to provide continuing assistance to the student beyond the preliminary meetings or refers the student to alternative sources of assistance that do not require parental notice or consent.

Standard I.1.3 Seeking Informed Consent

School psychologists ensure that an individual providing consent for school psychological services is fully informed about the nature and scope of services offered, assessment/intervention goals and procedures, any foreseeable risks, the cost of services to the parent or student (if any), and the benefits that reasonably can be expected. The explanation includes discussion of the limits of confidentiality, who will receive information about assessment or intervention outcomes, and the possible consequences of the assessment/intervention services being offered. Available alternative services are identified, if appropriate. This explanation of informed consent takes into account language and cultural differences, cognitive capabilities, developmental level, age, and other relevant factors so that it may be understood by the individual providing consent. School psychologists appropriately document written or oral consent. Any service provision by interns, practicum students, or other trainees is explained and agreed to in advance, and the identity and responsibilities of the supervising school psychologist are explained prior to the provision of services.

Standard I.1.4 Assent

School psychologists encourage a minor student's voluntary participation in decision making about school psychological services as much as feasible. Ordinarily, school psychologists seek the student's assent to services; however, it is ethically permissible to bypass student assent to services if the service is considered to be of direct benefit to the student and/or is required by law.

I.1.4a If a student's assent for services is not solicited, school psychologists nevertheless honor the student's right to be informed about the services provided.

I.1.4b When a student is given a choice regarding whether to accept or refuse services, the school psychologist ensures that the student understands what is being offered, honors the student's stated choice, and guards against overwhelming the student with choices that the student does not wish to make or is not able to make.

Standard I.1.5 Right to Refuse or Withdraw Consent

School psychologists respect the wishes of parents who object to school psychological services and attempt to guide parents to alternative resources. School psychologists allow parents to withdraw consent at any time without negative repercussions.

GUIDING PRINCIPLE I.2 PRIVACY AND CONFIDENTIALITY

School psychologists respect the right of persons to choose for themselves whether to disclose their private thoughts, feelings, beliefs, and behaviors.

Standard I.2.1 Sensitive Information

School psychologists minimize intrusions on privacy. They do not seek or store private information about clients that is not needed in the provision of services. School psychologists recognize that client–school psychologist communications intended only for the school psychologist are privileged in most jurisdictions. They do not disclose or store in education records any privileged information except as permitted by the mental health provider–client privilege laws in their state. School psychologists use a problem-solving model to consider carefully whether to share with third parties information that could put the student, family, or others at legal, social, or other risk. When school psychologists receive a report from a professional outside the school system that includes information that is intrusive of family privacy and not necessary for school decision making, the school psychologist considers whether returning the report to the maker with a request for redaction of the problematic information is the best course of action.

Standard I.2.2 Boundaries of Confidentiality

School psychologists inform students and other clients of the boundaries of confidentiality at the outset of establishing a professional relationship. They seek a shared understanding with clients regarding the types of information that will and will not be shared with third parties. However, if a child or adolescent is in immediate need of assistance, it is permissible to delay the discussion of confidentiality until the immediate crisis is resolved.

School psychologists recognize that it may be necessary to discuss confidentiality at multiple points in a professional relationship to ensure the client's understanding and agreement regarding how sensitive disclosures will be handled.

Standard I.2.3 Consent for Disclosure of Information

School psychologists respect the confidentiality of information obtained during their professional work. Information is not revealed to third parties without the agreement of a minor child's parent, legal guardian, or of an adult student, except in those situations in which failure to release information could result in danger to the student or others, or where otherwise required by law. Whenever feasible, the student's assent is obtained prior to disclosure of their confidences to third parties, including disclosures to the student's parents. When seeking consultation about a student or other client in a nonprivate forum (e.g., online discussion group), school psychologists ensure that the information they disclose is not sufficient to result in discovery of the client's identity.

Standard I.2.4 Need to Know

School psychologists discuss and/or release confidential information only for professional purposes and only with persons who have a legitimate need to know. They do so within the strict boundaries of relevant privacy statutes.

Standard I.2.5 Privacy Related to Sexual Orientation and Gender Identity and Expression

School psychologists respect the right of privacy of students, parents, and colleagues with regard to sexual orientation, gender identity, or transgender status. They do not share information about the sexual orientation, gender identity, or transgender status of a student (including minors), parent, or school employee with anyone without that individual's permission.

Standard I.2.6 Privacy of Health Information

School psychologists respect the right of privacy of students, their parents and other family members, and colleagues with regard to sensitive health information (e.g., presence of a communicable disease). They do not share sensitive health information about a student, parent, or school employee with others without that individual's permission (or the permission of a parent or guardian in the case of a minor). School psychologists consult their state laws and department of public health for guidance if they believe a client poses a health risk to others.

GUIDING PRINCIPLE I.3 FAIRNESS, EQUITY, AND JUSTICE

In their words and actions, school psychologists promote fairness and social justice. They use their expertise to cultivate school climates that are safe, welcoming, and equitable to all persons regardless of actual or perceived characteristics, including race, ethnicity, color, religion, ancestry, national origin, immigration status, socioeconomic status, primary language, gender, sexual orientation, gender identity, gender expression, disability, or any other distinguishing characteristics.

Standard I.3.1 Discrimination

School psychologists do not engage in or condone actions or policies that discriminate against persons, including students and their families, other recipients of service, supervisees, and colleagues based on actual or perceived characteristics.

Standard I.3.2 Correcting Discriminatory Practices

School psychologists strive to ensure that all children and youth have equal opportunity to participate in and benefit from school programs and that all students and families have access to and can benefit from school psychological services. They work to correct school practices that are unjustly discriminatory or that deny students or others their legal rights. School psychologists take steps to foster a school climate that is supportive, inclusive, safe, accepting, and respectful toward all persons, particularly those who have experienced marginalization in educational settings.

BROAD THEME II. PROFESSIONAL COMPETENCE AND RESPONSIBILITY

Beneficence, or responsible caring, means that the school psychologist acts to benefit others. To do this, school psychologists must practice within the boundaries of their competence, use scientific knowledge from psychology and education to help clients and others make informed choices, and accept responsibility for their work.

GUIDING PRINCIPLE II.1 COMPETENCE

To benefit clients, school psychologists engage only in practices for which they are qualified and competent. To maintain competence, they engage in continuing education. They understand that professional skill development beyond that of the novice practitioner requires a well-planned program of continuing professional development and professional supervision. In addition, within their work setting, they advocate for the resources and support necessary to maintain professional effectiveness and personal wellness.

Standard II.1.1 Practice in Area of Competence

School psychologists recognize the strengths and limitations of their graduate preparation and experience, engaging only in practices for which they are qualified. They enlist the assistance of other specialists in supervisory, consultative, or referral roles as appropriate in providing effective services. When no appropriate provider is available, school psychologists explain the limitations of their experience to parents and seek consultation, continuing professional development, and supervision as appropriate and necessary to ensure that students do not go without assistance.

Standard II.1.2 Personal Problems

School psychologists refrain from any work-related activity in which their personal problems may interfere with professional effectiveness. They seek consultation or other assistance when personal problems arise that threaten to compromise their professional effectiveness.

Standard II.1.3 Continuing Professional Development

School psychologists engage in continuing professional development. They remain current regarding developments in research, continuing professional development, and professional practices that benefit children and youth, families, and schools.

GUIDING PRINCIPLE II.2 ACCEPTING RESPONSIBILITY FOR ACTIONS

School psychologists accept responsibility for their professional work, monitor the effectiveness of their services, and work to correct ineffective recommendations.

Standard II.2.1 Accuracy of Documents

School psychologists review all of their written documents for accuracy, signing them only when correct. They may add an addendum, dated and signed, to a previously submitted document if information is found to be inaccurate or incomplete. In multidisciplinary reports or documents, school psychologists are ethically responsible only for the accuracy of their own contributions.

Standard II.2.2 Progress Monitoring

School psychologists ensure that the effects of their recommendations and intervention plans are monitored, either personally or by others. They revise a recommendation, or modify or terminate an intervention plan, when data indicate that the desired outcomes are not being attained. School psychologists seek the assistance of others in supervisory, consultative, or referral roles when progress monitoring indicates that their recommendations and interventions are not effective in assisting a client.

Standard II.2.3 Appropriateness of Recommendations

School psychologists accept responsibility for the appropriateness of their professional practices, decisions, and recommendations. They correct misunderstandings resulting from their recommendations, advice, or information and take affirmative steps to offset any harmful consequences of ineffective or inappropriate recommendations.

Standard II.2.4 Responsibility for Graduate Students' Work

When supervising graduate students' field experiences or internships, school psychologists maintain professional responsibility for their supervisees' work.

GUIDING PRINCIPLE II.3 RESPONSIBLE ASSESSMENT AND INTERVENTION PRACTICES

School psychologists maintain the highest standard for responsible professional practices in educational and psychological assessment and direct and indirect interventions. This guiding principle and its subsumed enforceable standards apply to school psychology assessment and intervention practices, including those that use technology such as computer-assisted and digital formats for assessment and interpretation, virtual reality assessment and intervention, distance assessment and telehealth intervention, or any other assessment or intervention modality.

Standard II.3.1 Considerations Prior to Disability Determination

Prior to the consideration of a disability label or category, the effects of current behavior management and/or instructional practices on the student's school performance are considered.

Standard II.3.2 Assessment Techniques

School psychologists use assessment techniques and practices that the profession considers to be responsible, research-based practice.

Standard II.3.3 Instrument Selection

School psychologists select assessment instruments and strategies that are reliable and valid for the examinee and the purpose of the assessment. When using standardized measures, school psychologists adhere to the procedures for administration of the instrument that are provided by the author or publisher of the instrument. If modifications are made in the administration procedures for standardized tests or other instruments, such modifications are identified and discussed in the interpretation of the results.

Standard II.3.4 Normative Data

If using norm-referenced measures, school psychologists choose instruments with norms that are representative, recent, and appropriate for the person being evaluated. School psychologists ensure that their supervisors are informed about the importance of using the most current version of published instruments.

Standard II.3.5 Digital Administration and Scoring

When using digitally administered assessments (e.g., computers, tablets, virtual reality) and/or computer-assisted scoring or interpretation programs, school psychologists choose programs that meet professional standards for accuracy and validity. School psychologists use professional judgment in evaluating the accuracy of digitally assisted assessment findings for the examinee.

Standard II.3.6 Variety of Sources of Data

A psychological or psychoeducational assessment is based on a variety of different types of information from different sources. No single test or measure is used to make broad determinations regarding disability identification or services needed.

Standard II.3.7 Comprehensive Assessment

Consistent with education law and sound professional practice, school psychologists ensure that students with suspected disabilities are assessed in all areas related to the suspected disability.

Standard II.3.8 Validity and Fairness

School psychologists conduct valid and fair assessments. They actively pursue knowledge of the student's disabilities and developmental, cultural, linguistic, and experiential background and then select, administer, and interpret assessment instruments and procedures in light of those characteristics. School psychologists ensure that assessment results are used to enhance learning opportunities for students.

Standard II.3.9 Interpreters

When interpreters are used to facilitate the provision of assessment and intervention services, school psychologists request the assignment of interpreters who are qualified and are acceptable to clients.

Standard II.3.10 Recommendations Based on Existing Records

It is permissible for school psychologists to make recommendations based solely on a review of existing records. However, they should use a representative sample of records and explain the basis for, and the limitations of, their recommendations.

Standard II.3.11 Interpretation of Results

School psychologists adequately interpret findings and present results in clear terms. They ensure that recipients understand assessment results so they can make informed choices.

Standard II.3.12 Intervention Selection

School psychologists use intervention, counseling and therapy procedures, consultation techniques, and other direct and indirect service methods that the profession considers to be responsible, evidence-based practice. They do so by using a problem-solving process to develop interventions that are appropriate to the presenting problems and consistent with data collected. Furthermore, preference is given to interventions described in the peer-reviewed professional research literature and found to be efficacious.

Standard II.3.13 Parental Involvement in Intervention Planning

School psychologists encourage and promote parental participation in designing interventions, including discussing with parents the recommendations and plans for assisting their children. When appropriate, this involvement includes linking interventions between the school and the home, tailoring parental involvement to the skills of the family, taking into account the ethnic/cultural values of the family, and helping parents gain the skills needed to help their children. Parents are informed of alternative sources of support available at school and in the community.

Standard II.3.14 Student Assent for Assistance

School psychologists discuss with students the recommendations and plans for assisting them. To the maximum extent appropriate, students are invited to participate in selecting and planning interventions.

GUIDING PRINCIPLE II.4 RESPONSIBLE SCHOOL-BASED RECORD KEEPING

School psychologists safeguard the privacy of school psychological records, ensure parents' access to the records of their own child, and ensure the access rights of adult students or otherwise eligible students to their own records.

Standard II.4.1 Notification of Rights and Responsibilities Regarding Records

School psychologists ensure that parents and adult students are notified of their rights regarding creation, modification, storage, and disposal of psychological and education records that result from the provision of services. Parents and adult students are notified of the electronic storage and transmission of personally identifiable school psychological records and the associated risks to privacy.

Standard II.4.2 Comprehensive Records

School psychologists create and/or maintain school-based psychological and education records with sufficient detail to be useful in decision making by another professional and with sufficient detail to withstand scrutiny if challenged in a due process or other legal procedure.

Standard II.4.3 Content of School Psychological Education Records

School psychologists include only documented information from reliable sources in a student's education records. School psychologists do not store in student education records any private information about students or their families that is not needed for the provision of school services. (See Ethics Standard II.4.8 Sole Possession Records.)

Standard II.4.4 Right to Inspect Records

School psychologists ensure that parents have appropriate access to the psychological and education records of their children, and that eligible students have access to their own records. Parents have a right to access any and all information that is used to make educational decisions about their children; eligible students have a right to access any and all information used to make educational decisions about them.

Standard II.4.5 Test Protocols

School psychologists respect the right of parents (and eligible students) to inspect, but not necessarily to copy, their child's (or their own) answers to school psychological test questions, even if those answers are recorded on a test protocol. School psychologists understand that the right of parents (and eligible students) to examine their child's (or their own) test answers may supersede the interests of test publishers.

Standard II.4.6 Access to Records by School Personnel

To the extent that school psychological records are under their control, school psychologists ensure that only those school personnel who have a legitimate educational interest in a student are given access to that student's school psychological records without prior parental permission or the permission of an adult student. This standard applies to access to physical and electronic records.

Standard II.4.7 Electronic Record Keeping

To the extent that school psychological records are under their control, school psychologists protect electronic files from unauthorized release or modification (e.g., by using passwords and encryption), and they take reasonable steps to ensure that school psychological records are not lost due to equipment failure.

Standard II.4.8 Sole Possession Records

It is ethically permissible for school psychologists to keep notes that are not accessible to others (i.e., sole possession records) to use as a memory aid. However, any and all information that is used to make educational decisions about a student is part of the student's education record and must be accessible to parents and adult students.

Standard II.4.9 Retention of Records

School psychologists, in collaboration with administrators and other school staff, work to establish district policies that are consistent with law and sound professional practice regarding the storage and disposal of school psychological records. They advocate for school district policies and practices that (a) safeguard the security of school psychological records while facilitating appropriate access to those records by parents and eligible students, (b) identify timelines for the periodic review and disposal of outdated school psychological records that are consistent with law and sound professional practice, (c) seek parental or other appropriate permission prior to the destruction or deletion of obsolete school psychological records of current students, and (d) ensure that obsolete school psychology records are destroyed or deleted in a way that the information cannot be recovered. In addition, school psychologists advocate for a school service delivery system in which working (not final) drafts of documents are not stored as student education records.

GUIDING PRINCIPLE II.5 RESPONSIBLE USE OF MATERIALS

School psychologists respect the intellectual property rights of those who produce tests, intervention materials, scholarly works, and other materials. They do not condone the use of restricted materials by unqualified persons.

Standard II.5.1 Test Security

School psychologists maintain test security, preventing the release of underlying principles and specific content that would undermine or invalidate the use of the instrument. School psychologists provide parents (and eligible students) with the opportunity to inspect and review their child's (or their own) test answers. When required by law or district policy, school psychologists may ethically provide parents (or eligible students) copies of their child's (or their own) completed test protocol. At the request of a parent (or eligible student), it is also ethically permissible to provide copies of test protocols to a professional who is qualified to interpret them.

Standard II.5.2 Use of Restricted Materials

School psychologists do not promote nor condone the use of restricted psychological and educational tests or other assessment tools or procedures by individuals who are not qualified to use them.

Standard II.5.3 Intellectual Property

School psychologists recognize the effort and expense involved in the development and publication of psychological and educational tests, intervention materials, and scholarly works. They respect the intellectual property rights and copyright interests of the producers of such materials, whether the materials are published in print or digital formats. They do not duplicate copyright-protected test manuals, testing materials, or unused test protocols without the permission of the producer.

BROAD THEME III. HONESTY AND INTEGRITY IN PROFESSIONAL RELATIONSHIPS

To foster and maintain trust, school psychologists must be faithful to the truth and adhere to their professional promises. School psychologists demonstrate integrity in professional relationships.

GUIDING PRINCIPLE III.1 ACCURATE REPRESENTATION

School psychologists are forthright about their qualifications, competencies, and roles.

Standard III.1.1 Accurate Presentation of Professional Qualifications

School psychologists accurately identify their professional qualifications to others. Competency levels, education, graduate preparation, experience, and certification and licensing credentials are accurately presented to clients, other recipients of services, potential and current employers, credentialing bodies, and public forums (e.g., on websites).

Standard III.1.2 Correcting Misperceptions

School psychologists correct any misperceptions of their qualifications. School psychologists do not represent themselves as specialists in a particular domain without verifiable graduate preparation and supervised experience in the specialty.

Standard III.1.3 Affiliation and Experience

School psychologists do not use affiliations with persons, associations, or institutions to imply a level of professional competence exceeding that which they have actually achieved. When submitting application to credentialing, licensing, or certification boards (e.g., National School Psychology Certification Board), school psychologists accurately report their graduate preparation and experience.

Standard III.1.4 Graduate Programs

Graduate program directors are responsible for ensuring that the descriptions of their programs accurately represent the nature of accreditation and/or approval by various bodies. If a program has not been awarded NASP approval, directors ensure that descriptions of the program do not imply that it meets NASP's *Standards for Graduate Preparation of School Psychologists.*

Standard III.1.5 Accuracy of Marketing Information

School psychologists ensure that announcements and advertisements of the availability of their publications, products, and services for sale are factual and professional.

GUIDING PRINCIPLE III.2 FORTHRIGHT EXPLANATION OF PROFESSIONAL SERVICES, ROLES, AND PRIORITIES

School psychologists are candid about the nature and scope of their services.

Standard III.2.1 Explanation of Services to Clients

School psychologists explain their professional competencies, roles, assignments, and working relationships to recipients of services and others in their work setting in a forthright and understandable manner. School psychologists explain all professional services to clients in a clear, understandable manner.

Standard III.2.2 Role Definition in Collaborative Work

School psychologists make reasonable efforts to become integral members of the client service systems (e.g., school-based teams) to which they are assigned. They establish clear roles for themselves within those systems while respecting the various roles of colleagues in other professions.

Standard III.2.3 Priority of Child Welfare

The school psychologist's commitment to protecting the rights and welfare of children and youth is communicated to the school administration, staff, and others as their highest priority in providing services. School psychologists are ethically obligated to speak up for the interests and rights of students and families even when it may be difficult to do so.

Standard III.2.4 Conflicts of Loyalties

School psychologists who provide services to several different groups (e.g., families, teachers, classrooms) may encounter situations in which loyalties are conflicted. As much as possible, school psychologists make known their priorities and commitments in advance to all parties to prevent misunderstandings. This is particularly important when the school psychologist is functioning in a nonclinical role, such as administrator, supervisor, or director.

GUIDING PRINCIPLE III.3 RESPECTING OTHER PROFESSIONALS

To best meet the needs of children, school psychologists cooperate with other professionals in relationships based on mutual respect.

Standard III.3.1 Cooperation With Other Professionals

To meet the needs of children and youth and other clients most effectively, school psychologists cooperate with other psychologists and professionals from other disciplines in relationships based on mutual respect. They genuinely consider input from nonschool professionals regarding student classification, diagnosis, and appropriate school-based interventions. They encourage and support the use of all resources to serve the interests of students. If a child or other client is receiving similar services from another professional, school psychologists promote the coordination of services.

Standard III.3.2 Referrals to Other Professionals

If a child or other client is referred to another professional for services, school psychologists ensure that all relevant and appropriate individuals, including the client, are notified of the change and reasons for the change. When referring clients to community-based professionals, school psychologists provide clients with lists of suitable practitioners from whom the client may seek services.

Standard III.3.3 Altering Reports

Except when supervising graduate students, school psychologists do not alter reports completed by another professional without their permission to do so.

GUIDING PRINCIPLE III.4 INTEGRITY IN RELATIONSHIPS

School psychologists avoid multiple relationships that diminish their professional effectiveness.

Standard III.4.1 Multiple Relationships and Professional Effectiveness

School psychologists refrain from any activity in which multiple relationships with a client or a client's family could reasonably be expected to interfere with professional effectiveness. School psychologists are cautious about business and other relationships with clients that could interfere with professional judgment and decision making or potentially result in exploitation of a client. When multiple relationships threaten to diminish professional effectiveness or would be viewed by the public as inappropriate, school psychologists ask their supervisor for reassignment of responsibilities, or they direct the client to alternative services.

Standard III.4.2 Multiple Relationships and Limited Alternative Services

In situations in which multiple relationships are unavoidable, such as when there is a lack of alternative service providers, school psychologists take the necessary steps to anticipate and prevent conditions that might compromise their objectivity, professionalism, or ability to render services. They establish and maintain clear professional boundaries, clarify role expectations, and rectify any misunderstandings that might adversely affect the well-being of a client or a client's family. In all cases, school psychologists prioritize the needs of the client and attempt to resolve any conflicts that emerge in a manner that provides the greatest benefit to the client.

Standard III.4.3 Harassment and Exploitation

School psychologists do not exploit clients, supervisees, or graduate students through professional relationships or condone these actions by their colleagues. They do not participate in or condone sexual harassment of children, parents, other clients, colleagues, employees, trainees, supervisees, or research participants.

Standard III.4.4 Sexual Relationships

School psychologists do not engage in sexual relationships with individuals over whom they have evaluation authority, including college students in their classes or program, or any other trainees or supervisees. School psychologists do not engage in sexual relationships with their current or former pupil-clients; the parents, siblings, or other close family members of current pupil-clients; or current consultees. Because they have an obligation to consider the well-being of all family members and to safeguard trust in psychologists, school psychologists are cautious about entering into sexual relationships with parents, siblings, or other close family members of the former client after the conclusion of the professional relationship.

GUIDING PRINCIPLE III.5 CONFLICTS OF INTEREST

School psychologists are forthright in describing any potential conflicts of interest that may interfere with professional effectiveness, whether these conflicts are financial or personal belief systems.

Standard III.5.1 Private Versus Professional Conduct

The *Principles for Professional Ethics* provides standards for professional conduct. School psychologists, in their private lives, are free to pursue their personal interests, except to the degree that those interests compromise trust in the profession or professional effectiveness.

Standard III.5.2 Separation of Personal Beliefs

School psychologists are aware of their own values, attitudes, and beliefs and how these affect their work with clients, families, school administration, staff, and the community. School psychologists' professional decisions, recommendations, and activities are guided by the evidence base and by best practices.

Standard III.5.3 Personal Beliefs and Experiences

School psychologists recognize when their own beliefs, attitudes, or experiences pose a barrier to providing competent services to a particular client or family. In such situations, the school psychologist obtains supervision that would allow them to provide quality services, if feasible. If not feasible, they ask for reassignment of the case to a different school psychologist, or they direct the client to alternative services and facilitate the transition to those services.

Standard III.5.4 NASP Leadership

NASP requires that any action taken by its officers, members of the Board of Directors or Leadership Assembly, or other committee or board members be free from the appearance of impropriety and free from any conflict of interest. NASP leaders recuse themselves from decisions regarding proposed NASP initiatives if they may gain an economic benefit from the proposed venture.

Standard III.5.5 Disclosure of Financial Interests

School psychologists' financial interests in products (e.g., tests, computer software, professional materials) or services can influence their objectivity or the perception of their objectivity regarding those products or services. For this reason, school psychologists are obligated to disclose any significant financial interest in the products or services they discuss in their presentations or writings, if that interest is not obvious in the authorship/ownership citations provided.

Standard III.5.6 Referrals and Remuneration

School psychologists neither give nor receive any remuneration for referring children and other clients for professional services.

Standard III.5.7 Remuneration for Data Sharing

School psychologists do not accept any remuneration in exchange for data from their client database without the permission of their employer and a determination of whether the data release ethically requires informed client consent.

Standard III.5.8 Practice in Both Public School and Private Settings

School psychologists who provide school-based services and who also engage in the provision of private practice services (dual setting practitioners) recognize the potential for conflicts of interest between their two roles and take steps to avoid such conflicts. Dual setting practitioners:

III.5.8a are obligated to inform parents or other potential clients of any psychological and educational services that are available to them at no cost from the schools prior to offering such services for remuneration;

III.5.8b may not offer or provide private practice services to a student (or their parents or family members) of a school or special school program where the practitioner is currently assigned unless these services are not available in the school setting;

III.5.8c may not offer or provide an independent evaluation as defined in special education law for a student who attends a local or cooperative school district where the practitioner is employed;

III.5.8d do not use tests, materials, equipment, facilities, secretarial assistance, or other services belonging to the public sector employer for private practice purposes unless approved in advance by the employer;

III.5.8e conduct all private practice outside of the hours of contracted public employment;

III.5.8f hold appropriate credentials for practice in both the public and private sectors.

BROAD THEME IV. RESPONSIBILITY TO SCHOOLS, FAMILIES, COMMUNITIES, THE PROFESSION, AND SOCIETY

School psychologists promote healthy school, family, and community environments. They assume a proactive role in identifying social injustices that affect children and youth and schools, and they strive to reform systems-level patterns of injustice. School psychologists who participate in public discussion forums, both in person and by electronic means, adhere to ethical responsibilities regarding respecting the dignity of all persons and maintaining public trust in the profession. School psychologists also maintain the public trust by respecting laws and encouraging ethical conduct. School psychologists advance professional excellence by mentoring less experienced practitioners and contributing to the school psychology knowledge base.

GUIDING PRINCIPLE IV.1 PROMOTING HEALTHY SCHOOL, FAMILY, AND COMMUNITY ENVIRONMENTS

School psychologists use their expertise in psychology and education to promote school, family, and community environments that are safe and healthy for children and youth.

Standard IV.1.1 Effective Participation in Systems

To provide effective services and systems consultation, school psychologists are knowledgeable about the organization, philosophy, goals, objectives, culture, and methodologies of the settings in which they provide services. In addition, school psychologists develop partnerships and networks with community service providers and agencies to provide seamless services to children and youth and families.

Standard IV.1.2 Promoting Systems Change

School psychologists use their professional expertise to promote changes in schools and community service systems that will benefit children and youth and other clients. They advocate for school policies and practices that are in the best interests of children and respect and protect the legal rights of students and parents.

GUIDING PRINCIPLE IV.2 RESPECT FOR LAW AND THE RELATIONSHIP OF LAW AND ETHICS

School psychologists are knowledgeable of and respect laws pertinent to the practice of school psychology. In choosing an appropriate course of action, they consider the relationship between law and the *Principles for Professional Ethics.*

Standard IV.2.1 Understanding Workplace Systems

School psychologists recognize that awareness of the policies, procedures, and legal requirements of their particular workplace is essential for effective functioning within those settings.

Standard IV.2.2 Intersection of Law and Ethics

School psychologists respect the law and the civil and legal rights of students and other clients. The *Principles for Professional Ethics* may require a more stringent standard of conduct than law, and in those situations school psychologists are expected to adhere to the Principles.

Standard IV.2.3 Conflicts Between Law and Ethical Principles

When conflicts between ethics and law occur, school psychologists take steps to resolve the conflict through positive, respected, and legal channels. If they are not able to resolve the conflict in this manner, they may abide by the law, as long as the resulting actions do not violate basic human rights.

Standard IV.2.4 Participation in Public Discourse

School psychologists may act as individual citizens to bring about change in a lawful manner. They identify when they are speaking as private citizens rather than as employees and when they are speaking as individual professionals rather than as representatives of a professional association. They also identify statements that are personal beliefs rather than evidence-based professional opinions.

GUIDING PRINCIPLE IV.3 MAINTAINING PUBLIC TRUST BY SELF-MONITORING AND PEER MONITORING

School psychologists accept responsibility for monitoring their own conduct and the conduct of other school psychologists to ensure that it conforms to ethical standards.

Standard IV.3.1 Application of Principles

School psychologists consult the *Principles for Professional Ethics* and thoughtfully apply them to situations within their employment role and context. In difficult situations, school psychologists use a systematic, problem-solving approach to decision making, including consulting experienced school psychologists, state associations, or NASP.

Standard IV.3.2 Resolution of Concerns With Colleagues

When a school psychologist suspects that another school psychologist has engaged in unethical practices, they attempt to resolve the suspected problem through a collegial problem-solving process, if feasible. If a collegial problem-solving process is not possible or productive, school psychologists take further action appropriate to the situation, including discussing the situation with a supervisor in the employment setting, consulting state association ethics committees, and, if necessary, filing a formal ethical violation complaint with state associations, state credentialing bodies, or the NASP Ethical and Professional Practices Board in accordance with their procedures.

Standard IV.3.3 Cooperation With the Ethics and Professional Practices Board

NASP members and NCSP credential holders cooperate with formal investigations of their conduct by NASP's Ethics and Professional Practices Board (EPPB). Consistent with the ethical guiding principle of accepting responsibility for their actions, school psychologists respond to ethical complaints personally (not through legal counsel or another third party) during the investigation phase unless the EPPB chair waives this requirement. School psychologists comply with the final disposition requirements imposed by the EPPB, if any.

GUIDING PRINCIPLE IV.4 CONTRIBUTING TO THE PROFESSION BY MENTORING, TEACHING, AND SUPERVISION

As part of their obligation to students, schools, society, and their profession, school psychologists mentor less experienced practitioners and graduate students to ensure high-quality services, and they serve as role models for sound ethical and professional practices and decision making.

Standard IV.4.1 Graduate Program Directors

School psychologists who serve as directors of graduate education programs provide current and prospective graduate students with accurate information regarding program accreditation, goals and objectives, graduate program policies and requirements, and likely outcomes and benefits.

Standard IV.4.2 Graduate Student Supervisors

School psychologists who provide direct supervision to practicum students and interns during field experiences are responsible for all professional practices of the supervisees. The field-based supervisor ensures that practicum students and interns are adequately supervised as outlined in NASP's *Standards for Graduate Preparation of School Psychologists*. Interns and graduate students are identified as such, and their work is cosigned by the supervising school psychologist.

Standard IV.4.3 Supervisor Responsibility

School psychologists who are faculty members at universities, those who supervise field experiences, and those who oversee the work of school psychology employees apply these ethical principles in their work with students and supervisees. They promote the ethical practice of graduate students and other supervisees by providing specific and comprehensive instruction, feedback, and mentoring. In addition, they advocate for optimal working conditions and continuing professional development opportunities for their supervisees.

GUIDING PRINCIPLE IV.5 CONTRIBUTING TO THE SCHOOL PSYCHOLOGY KNOWLEDGE BASE

To improve services to children and youth, families, and schools, and to promote the welfare of children, school psychologists are encouraged to contribute to the school psychology knowledge base by participating in, assisting in, or conducting and disseminating research.

Standard IV.5.1 Conducting Research

When designing and conducting research in schools, school psychologists choose topics and employ research methodology, research participant selection procedures, data-gathering methods, and analysis and reporting techniques that are grounded in sound research practice. School psychologists identify their level of graduate preparation and graduate degree to potential research participants.

Standard IV.5.2 Protecting the Rights of Research Participants

School psychologists respect the rights, and protect the well-being, of research participants. School psychologists obtain appropriate review and approval of proposed research prior to beginning their data collection.

IV.5.2a Prior to initiating research, school psychologists and graduate students affiliated with a university, hospital, or other agency subject to the U.S. Department of Health and Human Services (DHHS) regulation of research first obtain approval for their research from their Institutional Review Board for Research Involving Human Subjects (IRB) as well as the school or other agency in which the research will be conducted. Research proposals that have not been subject to IRB approval should be reviewed by individuals knowledgeable about research methodology and ethics and approved by the school administration or other appropriate authority.

IV.5.2b In planning research, school psychologists are ethically obligated to consider carefully whether the informed consent of research participants is needed for their study, recognizing that research involving more than minimum risk requires informed consent, and that research with students involving activities that are not part of ordinary, typical schooling requires informed consent. Consent and assent protocols provide the information necessary for potential research participants to make an informed and voluntary choice about participation. School psychologists evaluate the potential risks (including risks of physical or psychological harm, intrusions on privacy, breach of confidentiality) and benefits of their research and only conduct studies in which the risks to participants are minimized and acceptable.

Standard IV.5.3 Anonymity of Data

School psychologists may only use identifying case information in lectures, presentations, or publications when written consent to do so has been obtained from the client. Otherwise, they remove and disguise identifying case information when discussing assessment, consultation, or intervention cases.

Standard IV.5.4 Accuracy of Data

School psychologists do not publish or present fabricated or falsified data or results in their publications, presentations, and professional reports.

Standard IV.5.5 Replicability of Data

School psychologists make available their data or other information that provided the basis for findings and conclusions reported in publications and presentations, if such data are needed to address a legitimate concern or need and under the condition that the confidentiality and other rights of research participants are protected.

Standard IV.5.6 Correction of Errors

If errors are discovered after the publication or presentation of research or other information, school psychologists make efforts to correct errors by publishing errata, retractions, or corrections.

Standard IV.5.7 Integrity of Publications

School psychologists only publish data or other information that make original contributions to the professional literature. They do not report the same study in a second publication without acknowledging previous publication of the same data. They do not duplicate significant portions of their own or others' previous publications without permission of copyright holders.

Standard IV.5.8 Plagiarism

When publishing or presenting research or other work, school psychologists do not plagiarize the works or ideas of others. They appropriately cite and reference all sources, print or digital, and assign credit to those whose ideas are reflected. In inservice or conference presentations, school psychologists give credit to others whose ideas have been used or adapted.

Standard IV.5.9 Acknowledging Contributors

School psychologists accurately reflect the contributions of authors and other individuals who contributed to presentations and publications. Authorship credit is given only to individuals who have made a substantial professional contribution to the research, publication, or presentation. Authors discuss and resolve issues related to publication credit as early as feasible in the research and publication process.

Standard IV.5.10 Review of Manuscripts and Proposals

School psychologists who participate in reviews of manuscripts, proposals, and other materials respect the confidentiality and proprietary rights of the authors. They limit their use of the materials to the activities relevant to the purposes of the professional review. School psychologists who review professional materials do not communicate the identity of the author, quote from the materials, or duplicate or circulate copies of the materials without the author's permission.

TOPIC INDEX FOR THE ETHICAL PRINCIPLES

TOPIC INDEX FOR THE ETHICAL PRINCIPLES

Standard II.2.4 Responsibility for Graduate Students' Work

Standard III.1.1 Accurate Presentation of Professional Qualifications

Standard III.1.2 Correcting Misperceptions

Standard III.1.3 Affiliation and Experience

Standard III.1.4 Graduate Programs

Standard III.3.3 Altering Reports

Standard III.4.3 Harassment and Exploitation

Standard III.4.4 Sexual Relationships

Standard IV.4.1 Graduate Program Directors

Standard IV.4.2 Graduate Student Supervisors

Standard IV.4.3 Supervisor Responsibility

HIPAA

Standard I.2.6 Privacy of Health Information

Standard II.4.7 Electronic Record Keeping

Informed choices

Standard I.1.3 Seeking Informed Consent

Standard II.3.11 Interpretation of Results

Standard III.2.1 Explanation of Services to Clients

Standard III.4.2 Multiple Relationships and Limited Alternative Services

Instruments/tests

Standard II.3.3 Instrument Selection

Standard II.3.4 Normative Data

Standard II.3.5 Digital Administration and Scoring

Standard II.3.8 Validity and Fairness

Standard II.4.5 Test Protocols

Standard II.5.1 Test Security

Standard II.5.2 Use of Restricted Materials

Standard II.5.3 Intellectual Property

Interns

Standard I.1.3 Seeking Informed Consent

Standard II.2.4 Responsibility for Graduate Students' Work

Standard III.1.1 Accurate Presentation of Professional Qualifications

Standard III.1.2 Correcting Misperceptions

Standard III.1.3 Affiliation and Experience

Standard III.4.3 Harassment and Exploitation

Standard III.4.4 Sexual Relationships

Standard IV.4.2 Graduate Student Supervisors

Standard IV.4.3 Supervisor Responsibility

Interpretation of results

Standard II.3.3 Instrument Selection

Standard II.3.5 Digital Administration and Scoring

Standard II.3.6 Variety of Sources of Data

Standard II.3.8 Validity and Fairness

Standard II.3.11 Interpretation of Results

Interpreters

Standard II.3.9 Interpreters

Intervention

Standard I.1.1 When Consent Is/Is Not Required

Standard II.2.2 Progress Monitoring

Standard II.3.12 Intervention Selection

Standard II.3.13 Parental Involvement in Intervention Planning

Standard II.3.14 Student Assent for Assistance

Standard III.3.1 Cooperation With Other Professionals

Laws versus ethical principles

Standard IV.2.2 Intersection of Law and Ethics

Standard IV.2.3 Conflicts Between Law and Ethical Principles

LGBTQ

Standard I.2.5 Privacy Related to Sexual Orientation and Gender Identity and Expression

Standard I.3.1 Discrimination

Standard I.3.2 Correcting Discriminatory Practices

MTSS

Standard II.3.1 Considerations Prior to Disability Determination

Multiple relationships

Standard III.4.1 Multiple Relationships and Professional Effectiveness

Standard III.4.2 Multiple Relationships and Limited Alternative Services

Standard III.5.3 Personal Beliefs and Experiences

Standard III.5.8 Practice in Both Public School and Private Settings

Multiple roles

Standard III.2.4 Conflicts of Loyalties

Standard III.4.2 Multiple Relationships and Limited Alternative Services

Standard III.5.8 Practice in Both Public School and Private Settings

TOPIC INDEX FOR THE ETHICAL PRINCIPLES

Standard III.5.1 Private Versus Professional Conduct
Standard III.4.2 Multiple Relationships and Limited Alternative Services
Standard III.5.2 Separation of Personal Beliefs
Standard III.5.3 Personal Beliefs and Experiences
Standard III.4.3 Harassment and Exploitation
Standard III.4.4 Sexual Relationships
Standard IV.2.2 Intersection of Law and Ethics
Standard IV.2.3 Conflicts between Law and Ethical Principles
Standard IV.2.4 Participation in Public Discourse
Standard IV.3.1 Application of Principles

Progress monitoring

Standard I.1.1 When Consent Is/Is Not Required
Standard II.2.2 Progress Monitoring

Protocols

Standard II.4.5 Test Protocols
Standard II.4.9 Retention of Records
Standard II.5.1 Test Security
Standard II.5.3 Intellectual Property
Standard III.5.8 Practice in Both Public School and Private Settings

Psychological reports

Standard II.2.1 Accuracy of Documents
Standard II.2.2 Progress Monitoring
Standard II.2.3 Appropriateness of Recommendations
Standard II.3.3 Instrument Selection
Standard II.3.5 Digital Administration and Scoring
Standard II.3.6 Variety of Sources of Data
Standard II.3.8 Validity and Fairness
Standard II.3.11 Interpretation of Results
Standard II.4.6 Access to Records by School Personnel
Standard II.4.9 Retention of Records
Standard III.3.3 Altering Reports
Standard IV.4.2 Graduate Student Supervisors

Publications

Standard III.1.5 Accuracy of Marketing Information
Standard III.5.5 Disclosure of Financial Interests
Standard IV.5.1 Conducting Research
Standard IV.5.3 Anonymity of Data
Standard IV.5.4 Accuracy of Data
Standard IV.5.5 Replicability of Data
Standard IV.5.6 Correction of Errors
Standard IV.5.7 Integrity of Publications
Standard IV.5.8 Plagiarism
Standard IV.5.9 Acknowledging Contributors
Standard IV.5.10 Review of Manuscripts and Proposals

Qualifications

Standard II.5.2 Use of Restricted Materials
Standard III.1.1 Accurate Presentation of Professional Qualifications
Standard III.1.2 Correcting Misperceptions
Standard III.1.5 Accuracy of Marketing Information
Standard III.2.1 Explanation of Services to Clients

Recommendations

Standard II.2.3 Appropriateness of Recommendations
Standard II.3.8 Validity and Fairness
Standard II.3.10 Recommendations Based on Existing Records
Standard II.3.12 Intervention Selection
Standard II.3.13 Parental Involvement in Intervention Planning
Standard II.3.14 Student Assent for Assistance
Standard III.5.2 Separation of Personal Beliefs

Reevaluations

Standard II.3.10 Recommendations Based on Existing Records

Referrals to outside agencies

Standard I.1.2 Consent to Establish a School Psychologist–Client Relationship
Standard I.1.5 Right to Refuse or Withdraw Consent
Standard II.1.1 Practice in Area of Competence
Standard II.2.2 Progress Monitoring
Standard II.3.13 Parental Involvement in Intervention Planning
Standard III.3.2 Referrals to Other Professionals
Standard III.4.1 Multiple Relationships and Professional Effectiveness
Standard III.5.3 Personal Beliefs and Experiences
Standard III.5.6 Referrals and Remuneration
Standard III.5.8 Practice in Both Public School and Private Settings

Release of information

Standard I.2.3 Consent for Disclosure of Information

TOPIC INDEX FOR THE ETHICAL PRINCIPLES

Research

Standard IV.5.1 Conducting Research
Standard IV.5.2 Protecting the Rights of Research Participants
Standard IV.5.3 Anonymity of Data
Standard IV.5.4 Accuracy of Data
Standard IV.5.5 Replicability of Data
Standard IV.5.6 Correction of Errors
Standard IV.5.7 Integrity of Publications
Standard IV.5.8 Plagiarism
Standard IV.5.9 Acknowledging Contributors
Standard IV.5.10 Review of Manuscripts and Proposals

Responsibility

Standard II.2.1 Accuracy of Documents
Standard II.2.3 Appropriateness of Recommendations
Standard II.2.4 Responsibility for Graduate Students' Work
Standard III.1.5 Accuracy of Marketing Information
Standard III.4.2 Multiple Relationships and Limited Alternative Services
Standard IV.3.1 Application of Principles
Standard IV.3.2 Resolution of Concerns With Colleagues
Standard IV.3.3 Cooperation With the Ethics and Professional Practices Board

Right to refuse

Standard I.1.4 Assent
Standard I.1.5 Right to Refuse or Withdraw Consent

School climate

Standard I.3.1 Discrimination
Standard IV.1.1 Effective Participation in Systems

Self-care

Standard II.1.2 Personal Problems
Standard III.5.1 Private Versus Professional Conduct

Sensitive health information

Standard I.2.6 Privacy of Health Information
Standard II.4.3 Content of School Psychological Education Records

Sexual harassment

Standard III.4.3 Harassment and Exploitation
Standard III.4.4 Sexual Relationships

Sexual relationships

Standard III.4.3 Harassment and Exploitation
Standard III.4.4 Sexual Relationships

Social justice

Standard I.3.1 Discrimination
Standard I.3.2 Correcting Discriminatory Practices
Standard II.3.8 Validity and Fairness

Social media

Standard III.5.1 Private Versus Professional Conduct
Standard III.5.2 Separation of Personal Beliefs
Standard III.5.3 Personal Beliefs and Experiences
Standard III.4.3 Harassment and Exploitation
Standard IV.2.4 Participation in Public Discourse

Sole possession/private notes

Standard II.4.8 Sole Possession Records

Student records, General

Standard I.1.1 When Consent Is/Is Not Required
Standard I.2.1 Sensitive Information
Standard II.2.1 Accuracy of Documents
Standard II.3.10 Recommendations Based on Existing Records
Standard II.4.1 Notification of Rights and Responsibilities Regarding Records
Standard II.4.2 Comprehensive Records
Standard II.4.8 Sole Possession Records
Standard III.3.3 Altering Reports

Student records, Access to

Standard II.4.4 Right to Inspect Records
Standard II.4.5 Test Protocols
Standard II.4.6 Access to Records by School Personnel
Standard II.5.1 Test Security

Student records, Disposal/destruction of

Standard II.4.9 Retention of Records

Student records, Storage of

Standard II.4.3 Content of School Psychological Education Records
Standard II.4.7 Electronic Record Keeping

Supervision

Standard I.1.3 Seeking Informed Consent
Standard II.1.1 Practice in Area of Competence
Standard II.2.2 Progress Monitoring
Standard II.2.4 Responsibility for Graduate Students' Work
Standard III.1.1 Accurate Presentation of Professional Qualifications
Standard III.1.2 Correcting Misperceptions
Standard III.3.3 Altering Reports
Standard III.5.3 Personal Beliefs and Experiences
Standard III.4.4 Sexual Relationships
Standard IV.4.2 Graduate Student Supervisors
Standard IV.4.3 Supervisor Responsibility

Systems-level reform

Standard I.3.1 Discrimination
Standard I.3.2 Correcting Discriminatory Practices
Standard IV.1.1 Effective Participation in Systems
Standard IV.1.2 Promoting Systems Change
Standard IV.2.1 Understanding Workplace Systems

Technology

Standard II.2.1 Accuracy of Documents
Standard II.3.2 Assessment Techniques
Standard II.3.5 Digital Administration and Scoring
Standard II.4.1 Notification of Rights and Responsibilities Regarding Records
Standard II.4.7 Electronic Record Keeping
Standard II.4.9 Retention of Records
Standard III.5.1 Private Versus Professional Conduct
Standard IV.2.4 Participation in Public Discourse

Test security

Standard II.4.5 Test Protocols
Standard II.5.1 Test Security
Standard II.5.3 Intellectual Property

Index